GO TO HELP

31 STRATEGIES TO OFFER, ASK FOR, AND ACCEPT HELP

**DEBORAH GRAYSON RIEGEL, MSW
& SOPHIE RIEGEL**

Go To Help

First published in 2022 by

Panoma Press Ltd
a Rethink Press company
www.rethinkpress.com
www.panomapress.com

Book layout by Neil Coe.

978-1-784529-64-2

The right of Deborah Grayson Riegel and Sophie Riegel to be identified as the authors of this work has been asserted in accordance with sections 77 and 78 of the Copyright, Designs and Patents Act 1988.

A CIP catalogue record for this book is available from the British Library.

DEDICATED IN LOVING MEMORY TO

Joan Riegel

Nancy Strong

Shelly Goldin

and

Henry Grayson

Thank you for helping us in so many ways, big and small.

TABLE OF CONTENTS

INTRODUCTION

As the song goes in the Tony- and Pulitzer Prize-winning Broadway musical *Hamilton:* "The world turned upside down."

In March 2020, as COVID-19 spread across the globe, we all experienced our worlds turned upside down—our personal worlds, our work worlds, our school worlds, our parenting worlds, our health and mental health worlds, and more.

And one thing that many of us realized as we faced an uncertain, ever-changing future is that going it alone was not an option. Offering, asking for, and accepting help from others were vital to our physical and emotional survival.

We began to offer each other help in new ways, ranging from "I can help you set up your home office so that it doesn't look like a baby nursery" and "Do you want me to bring you a case of toilet paper if I can find some?" to "I hear that you're feeling isolated. Want to talk?"

We also needed to ask each other for help for things we couldn't have anticipated. "Could we please not do a video call, and just hop on the phone?" became a common request, as well as "Can you help me figure out how to teach math to my 5th grader?" And of course, with a degree of urgency, "Would you let me know if you find an open appointment to get a vaccination?"

If you're reading this book, it's probable that you survived *this* global pandemic because you offered, asked for, and accepted help. Congratulations!

And it's also likely that you want and need to get better at all three of these skills.

Every single one of us can and should become more "help fluent"—meaning that we have a wide range of ways that we can offer help to others, and ask for and accept help for ourselves.

This book will help you.

In Part 1, you'll be introduced to some surprising assumptions we make about what good help really looks like, and how what you *think* is helpful may not be. By putting aside your one or two "go-to" methods of helping—especially if they're not actually helping—you will learn some new approaches that can transform your impact and relationships at work and at home. You will also be encouraged to consider what asking for and accepting help means to your sense of self-efficacy, autonomy, and even your ego (which is not a dirty word). In addition, you'll get some support and direction about what to do if you're trying to help someone who doesn't want your help.

In Part 2, you'll be introduced to the 31 help strategies. You'll walk away with a deeper understanding of what helping strategy to use, when and with whom to use it (and when to skip it), as well as tips and tools for putting these new approaches into action. Whether you're trying to assist a colleague, a family member, a friend or someone else, you'll dramatically expand your skill sets for offering and delivering help that really helps.

Let's face it, we have more ahead of us that will require us to keep evolving in how to offer, ask for, and accept help: more adapting to a hybrid work environment and evolving expectations from today's workforce; more parenting in high-stress situations, as well as everyday parenting challenges; more participating in school that looks and feels different from even a few years ago; more supporting our friends and family through change, and change again.

Asking "How can I be most helpful to you?" is one of the most powerful questions you can ask someone, rather than assuming you already know. Then really listening to the answer is a gift to them—and to you. In addition, telling someone else exactly what would help you, as well as what doesn't feel like help, is a valuable way to build trusting, collaborative relationships with colleagues, friends, and family.

This book will help you be more skilled, strategic, and selective as you help others, as well as help yourself.

With gratitude to you, and to everyone who has helped you—and us—along the way.

Deborah Grayson Riegel and Sophie Riegel

August 2021

PART 1:

WHY OFFERING, ASKING FOR, AND ACCEPTING HELP IS HARD

—

CHAPTER 1:

HELP IS SURPRISINGLY COMPLEX

Think back to March 2020, when the COVID-19 outbreak officially became a global pandemic. Chances are, your boss told you not to come back into the office, and to figure out how to work from home. Or maybe you were an essential worker, and had to completely isolate yourself from family to do your job and keep them safe. Or perhaps you lost your job, and didn't know how you were going to make ends meet. Maybe your kids were sent home from school, and were expected to start attending classes online, if at all. Your parents started hearing the news about older adults being among the most vulnerable populations, and grew worried that they would contract the virus—and die. You couldn't see friends and family. Going to the grocery store became a terrifying outing, and even when you did go, the necessities like toilet paper and disinfectant were no longer available. You were trapped inside, worried about your present *and* your future.

ask yourself this: did you reach out to the local Global Pandemic Expert in your community for clear, concrete instructions on what to do, and how to get this solved?

The answer is no. Why? Because, first of all, you probably don't have a Global Pandemic Expert in your community. And secondly, because there weren't any clear, concrete instructions of what to do and how to get this solved.

This is because the global pandemic is an adaptive challenge rather than a technical one. And, in fact, many challenges where you want to offer help or ask for help are adaptive ones, too.

In their book *Leadership on the Line: Staying Alive Through the Dangers of Change*, Harvard Business School professors Ronald A. Heifetz and Marty Linsky identify adaptive challenges as problems, issues, or opportunities where your existing knowledge, skills, and expertise won't get it handled. They aren't clearly identified, and we all need to learn and experiment our way into a solution that doesn't yet exist. The solution requires developing new tools, habits, beliefs, priorities, values, roles, and relationships. And all of this learning and experimentation takes trial and error—and patience.

Like what?

- Like when Deb had to figure out how to redesign all of her workshops to be delivered virtually, while still maintaining her commitment to deep engagement and learning.

- Like when Deb's husband Michael had to figure out how to launch his new book and go on "book tour" when nobody was hosting live events.

- Like when Sophie was having panic attacks in high school, and needed to leave school early every day for a month, putting herself at risk for not graduating.

- Like when you had to figure out homeschooling your kids while working full time virtually.

- Like when you had to figure out how to take on a critical new project at work while onboarding three new hires and managing your current workload.

- Like when you had to figure out how to get your aging parent in declining health to accept the fact that they are losing their independence and need an aide at home.

There's no instruction manual, existing expertise, or straightforward help for any of these.

If there were, they'd be technical challenges.

Technical problems are easier to identify and recognize because you've likely seen them before, or someone with expertise or authority has. You may already know the steps for solving them, or you know someone who does. Their solutions are often quick, direct, and even easy. They don't require massive organizational change, and they also don't require significant emotional change, either.

When Deb's 83-year-old father-in-law Archie needed to take his arbitration practice online during the pandemic, he needed her technical help to set up a Zoom account and learn how to use its functions. By creating and following a checklist every time, he was able to get his business online quickly.

When Sophie's twin brother Jake fell down the stairs taking out the garbage and dislocated his shoulder, Deb took him to the Emergency Room where trained medical staff properly medicated him and then popped his arm back into the socket. (His mother Deb was asked to leave the room because dealing with squeamish parents was an adaptive challenge that the doctors didn't have time to deal with.)

And there's actually an important takeaway in that parenthetical: many problems for which we need to offer, ask for, and accept help have both technical *and* adaptive components.

When Deb was learning to drive at age 21, her instructor pointed out that she seemed very anxious to even turn on the ignition. When he asked her why, she responded, "I am afraid that the car is going to explode." Her driving instructor asked her whether she watched a lot of movies about organized crime, to which she responded, sheepishly, "Yes." He assured Deb that he had never seen an incident like that in his 20 years as an instructor, and advised her to stay away from those movies until she passed her driver's test. She agreed. Managing the anxiety about driving was the adaptive challenge; learning to drive was the technical part.

You probably recognize this combination in your own work and life.

It was a technical challenge for your kids to learn how to use the technology to attend school online, but it was an adaptive challenge for them to stay engaged and attentive. It's a technical challenge to take medicine to reduce your blood pressure, and it's an adaptive challenge to make diet, exercise, stress, sleep, and other lifestyle changes to keep you healthy over the long term. It's a technical challenge to learn your company's new customer relationship management software, but it's an adaptive challenge to keep your customers satisfied.

So, when it comes to offering, asking for, and accepting help, you need to recognize two things: first, that different kinds of challenges will require different kinds of help; and second, that even the process of offering, asking for, and accepting help is more adaptive than technical.

OFFERING HELP ISN'T ONE SIZE FITS ALL.

Let's start with offering help. Your colleague, friend, or family member has a problem, and you have a solution. Pretty straightforward, right?

Not necessarily.

Offering help is complex for a number of reasons. To start, it's easy to confuse technical challenges with adaptive ones, and so you may be offering the wrong kind of help.

Throughout his freshman year and first semester of his sophomore year in high school, Sophie's brother Jake seemed to be struggling in math. His test grades were mediocre, and his homework was riddled with errors. Deb and Michael arranged for him to go to school early mornings for extra help and tutoring, but it didn't boost his performance. Jake felt frustrated and hopeless, and so did his parents.

One day, Jake's math teacher, Mrs. A, called Deb and Michael in for a meeting.

"I've been watching Jake in class," she said, "and I think he actually knows his stuff."

"Then why is he doing so poorly in math?" Michael asked.

His teacher continued, "I think it's his confidence, not his competence." She went on, "As you know, I had Sophie in my class last year. Sophie is an excellent math student. I can't imagine it's easy for Jake to be Sophie's brother when it comes to math. I think he feels like he's being compared to Sophie."

It was quite a wake-up call for Deb and Michael. As parents of twins, they had done their best to shield their kids from comparisons, but at times, it was inevitable. And here was one of those times.

And they had offered him the wrong kind of help—instructional assistance for an emotional challenge.

As a result of this new awareness, Jake stopped getting technical help from his math teacher, and started getting adaptive help from his school psychologist to improve his feelings of confidence. By the end of the semester, Jake had brought his math average up from 70s to 90s.

Like most adaptive challenges, offering help often requires changes in beliefs, values, attitudes, and roles. You might have experienced this if you ever made the awkward transition from being someone's peer to becoming their manager. You likely wanted to be helpful to your former colleague/new direct reports, but felt unsure how to approach it because the new role felt uncomfortable.

This is exactly what Dave, a digital marketing professional, struggled with when he was promoted to a people manager role. He remarked, "I was Avi's 'Happy Hour' buddy last Friday, and on Monday, I was his new boss. How am I supposed to help him?"

Dave anticipated that offering managerial help to Avi would have both technical and adaptive challenges. The primary technical challenge is that Dave didn't suddenly have more expertise or knowledge than Avi had. A promotion hadn't made him a more experienced subject matter expert overnight. But the bigger issue was the adaptive one. When Dave thought about offering help to Avi, he wrestled with concerns like:

Is Avi resentful that I got promoted over him?

Will Avi see me as credible?

What if Avi doesn't want my help?

What if Avi actually knows more than I do?

How can I hold Avi accountable for results while still being his friend?

As you can imagine, this shift in role, responsibility, beliefs, and mindsets, made this new dynamic tricky for Avi and Dave. Dave struggled with how he could be a helpful and supportive manager to his new direct report, who was also his old friend.

Offering help can also be challenging because, while technical problems can be solved with outside expertise, adaptive problems need to be solved by the *person who has the problem*. (And if you're someone who has a habit of solving other people's problems, read that last sentence again.)

This is a conversation Deb has with almost every new coaching client. While some leaders have worked with coaches in the past, for those who are new to coaching, they often expect Deb to come to the coaching relationship with ready-to-go solutions. Like what?

Like…

"Here's how you can prevent people from needing your help and input during the workday so that you can focus on getting your work finished."

"Here's how you can convince your boss to promote you."

"Here's how to get your difficult colleague to stop being so argumentative and start listening to you with respect."

You know… just a few simple-to-solve problems!

When it comes to coaching, that's just not the way it works. Deb's role as a coach isn't to provide technical expertise for adaptive problems. Her role is to help the leader with the challenge explore their *own* mindsets, habits, perspectives, values, and behaviors so that they can experiment their way into a new, more helpful approach.

And you don't have to be a professional coach to recognize that one of the challenges in offering help is that, in many cases, you can't solve the problem *for* your friend, colleague, or family member. You can support them. You can cheerlead them. You can connect them to resources—if that's what they want. But the real work of getting it handled is theirs—whether they need help getting a new job, quitting smoking, leaving a toxic relationship, or anything else.

A final reason why offering help can be hard is because adaptive challenges can be easy to deny.

(Problem? What problem? I don't have a problem. Maybe YOU have a problem!)

Think about the people leader who says, "I don't have an anger management problem; I have a team of sensitive Millennials who only want positive feedback."

Think about your aging parent who says, "I don't have a vision problem; they're just printing everything smaller these days."

Think about your teenager who says, "I don't have a concentration problem; these teachers are just boring and don't know how to teach!"

Sound familiar?

It's hard to offer help to people who can't (or won't) acknowledge a problem. One contributing factor is known as "solution aversion," a term coined by Troy Campbell and Aaron Kay of Duke University.

When we are skeptical of or resistant to a solution, we tend to deny that the problem exists. In their research, Campbell and Kay presented research participants with two solution options for policy-related topics such as global warming, air pollution, and gun crime. While most participants agreed that these topics needed solving, they disagreed with a specific solution if they felt that solution was out of alignment with their ideological worldview.

But it doesn't have to be a big, heady, policy topic for solution aversion to show up in our own work and life. Deb, who long struggled with obsessive-compulsive disorder, avoided going to see a psychiatrist for years because she didn't want to take medication. She was averse to the solution, so she told herself, "I can live with this, it's no big deal." And yes, she *could* live with it and *did* live with it for decades. But it wasn't until her disorder became more difficult to live with than any imagined (or real) side effects of medication that she finally sought the help she needed (and she is thankful every single day that she got help).

Whether you're trying to help your team members through the emotional impact of a leadership transition, or help your daughter take accountability for her grades, or help your friend see that professional counseling might help his marriage, you can see that offering the right kind of help requires creativity, adaptability, and patience.

As helpful as you are, or want to be, it can help to know that offering help isn't always simple and straightforward.

ASKING FOR HELP CAN BE TRICKY, TOO.

It's not so simple to ask for help. Of course, if you're thinking about it solely in "technical" terms, asking for help is easy:

"I need help."

But, as you've probably guessed, asking for help is an adaptive challenge more than a technical one.

First of all, it can be hard to identify what the primary, first, or real problem is. Deb's client Andie, a senior scientific leader in a biotech, asked for help in having a difficult conversation with her boss. "I need to tell her that I can't do everything she's asking me to do. How do I tell her that I need her to take some work off my plate without her losing faith in me?"

Andie came to the coaching conversation with the assumption that she needed help addressing a tough topic with her boss. But Deb dug in a little deeper to identify what the first problem was to be addressed. "I'm happy to help you think through how to have that conversation," Deb offered, "and before we do that, can we first look at what's getting in the way of you getting things done?"

Andie initially bristled at the idea that she might have some time management challenges, but was willing to explore the topic with Deb. By the end of their hour-long coaching session, Andie recognized that she had three specific time management habits that she needed to improve: 1) analyzing how much time each of her tasks take to complete; 2) managing interruptions; and 3) delegating more work to team members. Andie committed to working on all three of those over the next six weeks before considering whether she needed to have that tricky conversation with her manager.

What Andie asked for help with wasn't wrong, it just wasn't the primary problem. And many of us ask for help based on what we *think* we need, rather than what we *actually* need.

Another reason it can be complicated to ask for help is that it may require a change in our mindset.

A mindset is a set of beliefs, perspectives, or attitudes we hold that drive the way we handle situations—the way we think about what is going on and what we should do. How we think and what we believe has a huge impact on our willingness to ask for help.

And it may be particularly challenging to ask for help if you have a fixed mindset rather than a growth mindset.

Stanford University psychologist Carol Dweck popularized ... idea of mindsets by contrasting different beliefs about where our abilities come from. If you have a *fixed mindset*, you tend to believe that skills and strengths are innate. You also believe that your talent alone leads to success—no effort required. You think of challenges as something to walk away from or work around. You measure yourself by your failures. You're either good at something or you're not.

And if you believe you're either good at something or you're not, then you probably believe that asking for help won't help.

In contrast, when you have a *growth mindset*, you believe that your skills, abilities, and talents can and will grow with time, experience, and yes—effort. You think of challenges as something to embrace—as an opportunity to improve. People with a growth mindset tend to show perseverance and resilience in the face of mistakes and setbacks. You are motivated to work harder.

People with fixed mindsets think, *I can either do it—or I can't do it.*

People with growth mindsets think, *I can either do it—or I can't do it* **yet!**

You can see the difference, right?

If you don't believe that you have the capacity, ability, and potential to develop and improve, you won't ask for help. In contrast, when you believe that you can embrace challenges and dilemmas as learning opportunities, then you will be more likely to ask for the help you need in support of your growth.

As hard as it may be to admit, high-school Sophie did not have a growth mindset at all. She would see any grade that wasn't 100 as a failure, any rejection from a scholarship as a personal attack, and she was afraid to be challenged because it might lead to less than perfect outcomes. It's hard to break the fixed mindset. And while Sophie has struggled with this mindset, she continues to remind herself that the only thing standing in the way of having a growth mindset is herself.

And by the way, it's important for you to hold a growth mindset about yourself as you learn to offer, ask for, and accept help. These aren't easy—and you *can* and *will* learn them!

Once you've recognized that asking for help doesn't mean you're not good enough or smart enough, you may also need to work on accepting the help that you've asked for or that's been offered to you.

Remember, one of the hallmarks of adaptive challenges is that it requires us to shift values, beliefs, roles, and relationships. This can be hard when it comes to accepting help, and it is necessary for any of us to get the support we need.

Six weeks into their coaching relationship, Deb noticed that Pilar, a global leader in a financial services firm, wasn't honoring the commitments to behavior change she had made to herself. In other words, she had *asked* for help but wasn't accepting the help.

Deb noticed this aloud to Pilar, and asked if she'd be willing to explore what might be getting in the way. Pilar agreed, and Deb helped her unpack the following self-awareness.

- **Pilar's values:** Autonomy ("I want to do things independently"), Recognition ("I want other people to notice and appreciate what I do"), and Ambition ("I want to get ahead").

- **Her beliefs about accepting help**: "I should know how to do all of this by myself."

- **Her role in accepting help**: "I am the helper among my friends and family. Who am I if I am not the helper?"

- **Her relationship to accepting help**: "I am going to feel dependent on someone else for my success."

It became clear to Pilar that she had some limiting beliefs and relationships when it came to accepting help that were getting in her way. It was hard for her to accept help when she valued doing things independently, believed she should be able to do things herself, saw herself as the helper rather than a "helpee," and conflated accepting help with being dependent.

For homework, Pilar rewrote these statements using a "yes, and…" approach, to create space for her current beliefs, and some newer ones. She didn't want to feel like she needed to change her identity to change her approach.

Here's what she came up with that allowed her strategy to evolve while preserving her identity:

- **Values:** Autonomy ("I want to do things independently, **and accepting help will give me the opportunity to be more independent down the road**"), Recognition ("I want other people to notice and appreciate what I do, **and accepting help now will help me have greater recognition later**"), and Ambition ("I want to get ahead, **and accepting help will get me there faster**").

- **Beliefs about accepting help**: "I should know how to do all of this by myself, **and since I don't yet, I might as well take the help that's being offered to me.**"

- **Role in accepting help:** "I am the helper among my friends and family. Who am I if I am not the helper? **I am both a helper and a helpee. And learning to accept help will make me a better helper, too!**"

- **Relationship to accepting help**: "I am going to feel dependent on someone else for my success. **And I can accept help while fully owning my successes.**"

Those shifts in thinking helped Pilar *feel* and ultimately *be* more open to accepting help. Six months later, Pilar was promoted to a senior global leadership position. Accepting help helped her get there.

And so did her patience. Accepting help doesn't mean that your problem will be instantly solved. If it did, people would be more fit after their first session with a trainer, or be better writers after their first round of edits. Deb's friend Juliann has helped her with a full office organizational overhaul several times, and Deb, admittedly, is not much better at keeping the clutter at bay. Accepting help can also require us to accept that change is going to take a while.

Sophie, like a lot of people, is not the most patient person. She likes her work to be done quickly, others to follow through on their commitments in a timely manner, and is a strong believer that early is on time and on time is late. Unfortunately for her, when she was having panic attacks daily when she was 16, she knew that the only possible solution was one that would not work instantly: medication.

"Your medication won't start kicking in for about four to six weeks," her psychiatrist told her.

"Four to six weeks? Isn't there something that will work for me now?" Sophie asked.

As it turned out, that if Sophie wanted to calm her anxiety, she would need to be patient. Sure enough, four to six weeks later, Sophie's panic attacks became less frequent. But this only happened because Sophie was willing to wait and accept that change takes time.

It's not just about accepting that some help may take some time to stick. When it comes to accepting help, you first need to believe that you are worthy of help and that you can be helped.

And in case you're thinking to yourself at this point, *Who knew that help was so hard?* there is some good news. Some help can be simple, fast, and easy—especially when it's a technical problem.

During the pandemic, Sophie kept busy by working on 1000-piece jigsaw puzzles. Once she found the missing puzzle piece that snapped into its spot, she considered that section solved and moved on to the next section.

A technical challenge is like a puzzle. If you locate the missing piece and snap it in, you can move on.

Sometimes that missing puzzle piece is expertise, knowledge, or experience. Before Deb signed her first book contract, she had a literary attorney review it to make sure it represented her interests. It would have made no sense for her to try to figure it out herself. When Sophie's car kept dying, she took it to a mechanic who quickly diagnosed that it needed a new battery, and replaced it. Sophie could have done this herself (well, probably not), but it was safer, faster, and easier to have a professional handle it.

A missing puzzle piece could also be a resource, like time, energy, people, or money. After the financial crash in 2008, Deb and Michael realized that they needed financial help to cover their mortgage for the next three months. They called Michael's parents, Joan and Archie, to come over for a talk, and when they arrived, Michael asked them for a short-term loan. To their surprise, Archie started to laugh. When Deb asked why he was laughing, he replied, "We were worried it was a real problem, like someone was sick or you were getting a divorce. This is an easy problem to solve."

Of course, it pays to note that money is a technical problem to solve if you can easily access the money; it's an adaptive one if you can't. And it also becomes an adaptive challenge if there are strings attached to that money.

Deb and Michael accepted their help, and with no strings attached, they repaid it within the year. Technical problem; technical solution.

Your missing puzzle piece may be a deadline extension to complete a project, or needing ten seasonal employees to get your business through the holiday rush. If it can be solved with quick, concrete solutions, then it can be easier to offer, ask for, and accept help. Like "we need to translate this document into six languages for our global teams" (and we know who can do it, and can cover the costs). Like "turn down the oven from 400 to 350 degrees after 15 minutes so you don't burn the pie crust." Or, when Sophie started her thrift clothing resale business, identifying which online resale platform would offer her the most profits for her efforts.

Offering, asking for, and accepting help is often complex, sometimes tricky, occasionally simple—and almost always worth it. And, like so many other skills in work and life, you will get better at it with experience, practice, and patience.

CHAPTER 1: REVIEW AND REFLECT

REVIEW:

- Some help requires a technical solution, which is like looking for a missing puzzle piece. Once you locate the missing piece and snap it in, you can move on.

- Most help requires an adaptive approach, meaning the person who needs help may need to experiment with new mindsets, behaviors, habits, and approaches to get their problem solved.

- Getting better at offering, asking for, and accepting help is an adaptive challenge, which will take practice and patience. And it's worth it!

REFLECT:

- Think about someone you'd like to offer help to on a particular challenge they're facing. What parts of their challenge do you think are technical, and which ones are adaptive?

- Consider a dilemma that you're facing right now. What are the technical elements? And which ones are adaptive?

CHAPTER 2:

YOUR GO-TO WAY OF HELPING ISN'T ENOUGH

They thought they were helping me...
but I didn't need help.
They thought they were fixing me...
but I wasn't broken.
They thought they were watering me...
but they were drowning me.

Steve Maraboli, United States Air Force Military Police

As humans, we have a natural tendency to see a problem and try to fix it. Or even more commonly, we see a person with a problem and try to fix *them*. And this makes sense that, if we see something wrong, our instincts tell us to make it right. But the way we go about "making it right" may have negative impacts on the person we are trying to help, despite our intentions being good.

And, if we only have one or two ways of being helpful, we are probably hindering others more than actually helping them—as well as holding ourselves back from expanding our range. This is why you need to become "help fluent"—have a wide range of different strategies, options, and approaches to helping others.

Take Sophie's dad and Deb's husband, Michael, for example. He is a trained civil engineer and his education and career taught him that when there is a problem, there must be a solution. A crumbling bridge can be rebuilt. A burst water pipe can be soldered back together. At home, he is Mr. Fix-it. The toilet is clogged? He plunges it. There's a board in the deck sticking out? He nails it back in. His go-to way of helping is to fix it. But this kind of help doesn't work in all situations.

When Sophie was in middle school, she was diagnosed with obsessive-compulsive disorder and trichotillomania, a hair-pulling disorder. In high school, she was diagnosed with panic disorder and generalized anxiety disorder. Because of this, Sophie was dealing with crippling anxiety and panic attacks on a daily basis. She always went to Deb for support with her mental health because Deb was able to listen, empathize, and ask her what kind of help she needed. However, when Deb traveled for work, Sophie had no choice but to turn to her dad.

Michael's go-to way of helping, fixing it or telling someone how to fix it made it hard for Sophie to get the support she needed. In fact, Sophie's relationship with Michael suffered. She did not want to go to him when she was feeling anxious or upset because she knew that would activate Mr. Fix-it. Michael was frustrated with this, knowing that he wanted to help, and believing that he could help. It wasn't until Sophie and her dad had a long overdue talk about the discrepancies between what Sophie needed and what Michael was providing that Michael understood that despite his good intentions (which no one ever doubted), he was having a negative impact.

YOUR INTENTIONS ARE GOOD BUT YOUR IMPACTS ARE MIXED.

When you offer help, especially offering a "fix-it" kind of help, you have good intentions. Your drive and desire to help others get out of a sticky situation is what makes you a prosocial being—someone whose behavior is positive, helpful, and intended to promote social acceptance, connection, and friendship. That's why when Michael tried to fix things about Sophie's mental health, she trusted that his intentions were positive, even though the impact was negative.

If you are on the receiving end of someone interpreting your desire for help as a need to have your problem fixed, you may feel misunderstood. It's an interesting phenomenon to reflect on. The most common ways in which people try to help is to fix it or tell you how to fix it. And yet, this kind of help is often the least helpful.

If you know that *you* don't like it when someone tries to fix your problem, why do you then go try to fix *someone else's* problem when they ask for help?

Often, we think that when helping, it is our intentions that matter most. You know the phrase "It's the thought that counts"? Your mom gets you an ugly necklace from a boutique she went to, and all you can say to yourself is, "Well, it's the thought that counts, right?" Or your kids ask you what you want for your birthday and you say, "I'll love anything you get me because it's the thought that counts." (We all know you don't want a macaroni necklace, even if it's nicer than the necklace your mother got you.) And when we receive a gift, it matters that someone else thought of us—and that's part of what makes that gift special.

When it comes to helping others, however, it is *not* the thought that counts, but the impact that we have on the person we're trying to assist.

If you go to the barber and get a haircut, does it matter that he tried his best if it looks like a three-year-old cut your hair with a pair of dull scissors? If you go to a restaurant, does it matter that the chef made you his best eggplant parmesan if you ordered a Greek salad? It's clear that the impact matters most in these situations, and the same thing is true when we are offering, asking for, or receiving help.

If someone in your work or life has a challenge, dilemma, or issue that they're wrestling with, and you try to fix it for them when that's not what they want or need, they are likely to feel resentful, frustrated, insecure, overwhelmed, or worse. In addition, you will begin to erode the trust in your relationship, which, over time, can mean that they don't even come to you for help in the first place.

And yet, we still persist. Why?

WE ARE REWARDED FOR OUR GO-TO HELPING APPROACH.

You know about endorphins, right? They are chemicals produced by your nervous system to cope with pain or stress. Sophie experiences a rush of endorphins (known as a "Runner's High") when she goes for a jog outside. The good news for people like Deb (running? yuck!) is that you don't need to be an athlete to get that good feeling. You have likely already experienced a "Helper's High," which is the exhilaration you feel when you help someone else. Doing acts of kindness and giving to others produces a neurochemical reward, similar to a dose of morphine.

But wait! There's more! Let's not forget another favorite, feel-good chemical: serotonin. Serotonin gets released when we feel important and powerful, as well as when we dominate others. And helping someone else can make us feel important and powerful, and also make them feel dominated by us, especially if you aren't yet using the healthier helping approaches in this book.

So what's the downside to these neurochemical rewards? It's that we experience positive emotions *regardless of whether the other person experiences you as helping them.* You register "I'm helping! I'm important! I'm powerful" based on your intentions and actions, not on the impact of those actions.

And the list of rewards goes on.

- Our egos get rewarded when we conflate our helping strength with what people actually need: "Look how much people need me to help them make hard decisions!" (Even if they don't.)

- We save time when we don't have to learn new helping approaches. "I could point out the upside of any situation in my sleep!"

- We avoid decision fatigue when we have no decisions to make about how to help someone: "You called me, so I assume you want some advice, right?"

- We experience less emotional and cognitive burden when we only help in one or two ways: "I'm happy to give you direct feedback, but if you're looking for empathy, go talk to Amy."

But before you start blaming yourself for being stuck in your helping ways, take note: you probably come from a long line of people in your personal and professional lives who weren't "help fluent" either.

YOU LEARNED FROM YOUR ROLE MODELS.

Many important and influential people in your life were terrific at helping you, but were probably unskilled at helping you in a wide range of ways. Think about your parents, and how they helped you most often. Did they:

- Step in and fix things for you?

- Listen without judgment?

- Empathize?

- Teach you how to do things on your own?

- Hold you accountable for your actions?

- Connect you to people in their network?

Chances are, they did one or two of those things very well—but not all, or even many.

Now think about your first, current, or best boss at work. What was their go-to helping approach? Maybe it was giving you timely constructive feedback, but you were also yearning for some positive feedback, too. Or they helped you set clear goals, but weren't consistent in helping you anticipate the inevitable obstacles that would come up along the way.

Our teachers are a part of this system, too. Some are excellent at explaining concepts or ideas to a struggling student, but not good when it comes to listening without giving advice. Deb's math teacher in middle school helped her become an excellent math student by having high expectations and holding the bar high for her. What she didn't bring to the equation was empathy. Sophie's English teacher was great at giving examples of what good writing looks like. What she didn't provide was direct feedback on how to make her writing better.

When it comes to helping others, most of us have one or two strategies because we've been taught, parented, and managed by people who also have one or two strategies. And it's hard to learn something you haven't seen in practice.

WE ALSO DON'T KNOW WHAT WE DON'T KNOW.

We all have blind spots. We are often unable to see that the way to help someone is something we don't know how to do *yet*. Or we don't realize that the way we know how to help isn't helpful, especially when we've historically confused good intentions with good impacts.

Think about yourself driving a car. You are going down the highway and you want to change lanes. The car in the lane beside you is in your blind spot, so if you go to change lanes, you will hit it. Luckily, your car beeps and tells you it is not safe to change lanes. The beep lets you know that there is something in your blind spot. Feedback is that beep. You need feedback to avoid getting into a crash, or, in terms of help, you need it to avoid offering help that is misguided, uncalled for, or simply unsupportive. If you don't ask for and receive feedback, you will not know where your blind spots are, which could lead to (metaphorical) crashes and clashes with those whom you want to assist.

What makes this particularly challenging is that it's rare for someone to tell us in a direct and timely manner that our help isn't helping. Few people are *volunteering* feedback on the kind of help we are giving because it feels awkward and uncomfortable, and sometimes, ungrateful. Furthermore, even fewer of us are asking "Hey, how helpful was my help?" As a result, we continue to help in unhelpful ways.

If you'd like to get some feedback about your helping approaches, here are three simple questions you can ask:

- What have I said or done in the past that felt most helpful to you?

- What have I said or done in the past that felt unhelpful to you?

- How could I be more helpful to you in the future?

STOP DEFAULTING TO FIXING THINGS FOR PEOPLE OR TELLING THEM HOW TO FIX IT.

"Just tell me what to do!"

Admittedly, there are times when your kid, your partner, or your colleague will throw their hands up, and ask you to dictate the next steps. However, too often we *imagine* (or hope) that this is what someone is asking us to do—step in and save the day—rather than stopping to ask them, "What kind of help would be most helpful to you right now?"

Most people do not want you to fix things for them, or tell them how to fix it.

Why? Because you taking over can rob them of their sense of autonomy, independence, and agency. It can create a dependency that impedes their growth, learning, and development, and an interdependency where you need to be needed by them.

Of course, this impact can be different when living or working with people from around the globe. Each culture has its own norms for how people should behave with each other, and that extends to offering, asking for, and accepting help. (For a deeper understanding of these global and cultural distinctions, check out Erin Meyer's book *The Culture Map: Breaking Through the Invisible Boundaries of Global Business*, or Andy Molinsky's book *Global Dexterity: How to Adapt Your Behavior Across Cultures without Losing Yourself in the Process*.)

Nevertheless, the majority of the people we live with or work with care about being self-sufficient and that requires them to fix their own problems, even if it also means they make mistakes.

FIXING IT FOR THEM CREATES COMPLACENCY AND COMPLIANCE.

One of Deb's favorite quotes is "Nobody ever washes a rental car," (and if you do, the authors are both impressed and a bit concerned). Why don't you wash your rental car? Because you don't own it. You're not committed to the long-term appearance of a car that isn't yours. You know that a) someone else will wash it, and b) you are only using it for a short period of time, and it's not worth your investment of time, money, or energy.

Let's think about someone else's problem as a car. When you fix it for them, you are making their problem a rental car. They won't feel committed to learning how to fix it themselves—they will not wash it. They become complacent, or compliant, or dependent on you to wash their car for them so they can return the car faster—to solve the problem faster.

What you really want to do when helping people is to help them think of their problem as a car they own. No one is going to wash it for them. If they don't take care of it, it will be costly. They cannot return the car whenever they decide they don't want to deal with it anymore.

Sticking with the car theme, when Sophie and Jake were learning how to drive, the car battery died often. Michael continued to jump the car for them, explaining along the way how to do it but not actually giving them the chance to do it on their own. Recently, when the car died again, Michael became frustrated that Sophie and Jake needed his help. "I told you how to fix it," he would say. "You should know how to do it by now." The truth is, though, Sophie and Jake had become complacent. There was no need for them to commit to learning how to fix it themselves if they knew their dad was always going to fix it for them. Michael told the kids, through frustration (because of his perceived wasted time and energy), that he was going to show them how to do it one more time but after that, they would have to do it on their own. Telling Sophie and Jake that he was no longer going to fix it for them turned the rental car into their own car, one which they would have to take care of themselves, or it would not work. This made them committed to learning how to jump the car, and get rid of their complacency and dependence on their dad. And more than that, Michael's frustration disappeared.

You may see this dynamic at work, too. Your boss tells you not just *what* to do (say, plan a professional development program for mid-level managers), but what the program needs to include, when it should run, who should teach the courses, how to do the internal marketing, etc. Once that happens, you're no longer owning it. You're just going along for the ride.

Does this sound familiar—either as something you've had done to you, or something you've done to others? You're certainly not alone. But you're already too far into this book not to do something about it!

As Marshall Goldsmith highlights in his best-selling book *What Got You Here Won't Get You There: How Successful People Become Even More Successful,* when you tell someone what to do (or how to make what they're already doing even better) you may have improved the content of their idea by 5–10%, but you've reduced their commitment to executing it by 50%. Why? Because telling them what to do takes away their ownership of the idea. Have you added value? Perhaps. And have you done it at the cost of their commitment? Almost certainly.

Think about someone at work whom you've been trying to help with a project, problem, or opportunity. Have you been "helping" by fixing it for them or telling them how to fix it? If so, try shifting from telling to asking: "What could you do to make this even more

successful/viable/profitable?" And then stop talking, an
listening.

SOMETIMES FIXING IT OR TELLING THEM HOW TO FIX IT IS THE RIGHT WAY TO HELP.

(*Now* you tell me?)

Admittedly, fixing things for someone else doesn't always have a
negative impact, especially if it's a technical challenge. Sometimes,
it's exactly what's needed. Now the question is: how do you know?

Here are some indicators that you may need to step in:

1. The other person lacks specific skills or knowledge.

2. The other person doesn't need to learn how to do this and/or won't need to do this again.

3. Compliance is more important than commitment.

4. When a decision needs to be made immediately.

5. The other person doesn't have the resources they need to do it themselves (time, money, energy, emotional or cognitive capacity, etc.)

6. When you aren't willing to commit yourself to their development.

7. This task is urgent.

8. This task poses a financial, reputational, or other significant risk.

9. There's a crisis, or you're trying to prevent a crisis.

10. There is a right way and a wrong way to get it done.

When it comes to helping others, you will likely need to unlearn some old habits to help the people you work with and live with to master their challenges and dilemmas. And no worries—new, healthier helping habits are just a few pages away!

YOUR OPEN-DOOR POLICY ISN'T AS HELPFUL AS YOU THINK.

"Call me if you need anything."

"I'm here for you."

"My door is always open."

You've said one (or all) of these, correct? Of course you have. And you said them because you want people to know that they can reach out to you for anything. However, when you say this, you are actually *decreasing* the likelihood that someone will come to you for help. Why? Because you leave too much up to their interpretation of what you're really offering, too many options on the table, and too many decisions for the other person to make.

When Sophie was in high school, her math teacher told the class at the beginning of the year that if students needed anything, they could come to her. When Sophie was diagnosed with panic disorder that same year and desperately needed support from her teachers, she was hesitant to go to them. When Deb asked her why she wouldn't go to her math teacher, Mrs. D, who specifically said that students could talk to her about anything, here's what Sophie said: "She didn't mean I could talk to her about *this*. She probably meant I could come to her with math-related problems." The word "anything" was so broad that Sophie believed that her teacher didn't really mean it. (As Sophie would come to learn, Mrs. D really did mean *anything!*)

When you tell someone to come to you for anything, too many of the people you're trying to help may think to themselves, *Well, they didn't mean I should come to them for **this** problem.*

Another misstep you might make is asking "How can I help you?" While you want to give people the opportunity to tell you what would be most helpful to them, you don't want to paralyze them with choices. When you ask them this, people often do not know either a) what they need, or b) what options they have. As the saying goes, "a confused mind buys nothing." When offering help, you need to be specific so that your colleague or kid or friend isn't wondering what options are available. Blanket statements leave people wondering and questioning whether they can come to you, and what to ask for.

Here's how you can offer help specifically:

"Would making a pros and cons list be helpful to you right now?"

"Call me if you want me to bring you a lasagna, or pick up your kids from school, or just stop by for a hug. Also, please don't feel obligated to call me!"

"If you're feeling depressed or anxious, no matter what time of day, please come knock on my door."

"How would you feel if I just listened to you right now? Or do you need something else?"

CHAPTER 2: REVIEW AND REFLECT

 REVIEW:

- You have been rewarded for the one or two ways you are most helpful, which means that you may not have cultivated additional helping skills.

- You are likely to assess the quality of your help based on your intention, but the person you're helping is evaluating your impact.

- Fixing it for someone or telling them how to fix it are most people's default helping strategies, but these should be used sparingly and strategically.

 REFLECT:

- Think about someone who may benefit from help. What can you offer to them other than fixing it for them or telling them how to fix it?

- Remember a time when you asked someone for help, and they stepped in by fixing it for you or telling you how to fix it—and that wasn't what you needed. What was the impact on you? What approach(es) would have been more helpful?

CHAPTER 3:

YOU CAN BE BOTH SELECTIVE AND HELPFUL

Let's say that you've gotten really good at asking for help. You've changed your mindset about asking, you've figured out what kind of help you need, you know who to ask and how to ask them.

There's still one more skill to develop so that you're still not overworked, overwhelmed, and overextended. What's that?

Only offer the kind of help that you can really, truly give right now.

Yes, asking for help is important. And knowing what help you can and should give to others is just as critical, too. If you say yes to every request, you won't actually be helpful to others—and you won't be helping yourself either. As Adam Grant describes it, you want to be "other-ish," rather than selfless.

HOW TO OFFER HELP.

Here are three criteria to help you think through the kind of help you can and should offer:

1. **Determine what you're able to do.** This means knowing your strengths and weaknesses in giving help. Deb is highly skilled at listening without judgment, but when it comes to helping someone get organized, she's not your go-to gal. Sophie is exceptional at helping someone see the details, but she won't be your first call if you need someone to empathize with you when you've made a mistake and are struggling to deal with the consequences. You may be terrific at helping someone make an action plan, or consider their pros and cons, or empathize with their stress about parenting young kids, but you may not be the right person to point them to external resources, or to help them create evaluation criteria, or support them in thinking about what *is* working rather than what isn't. We can't all be skilled at everything, and that's OK.

Only offer help or accept a request for help for the kind of help you're capable of delivering. And, if you decide that you're using this as an opportunity to learn new helping skills (like "I really want to practice listening without advising"), let your friend, family member, or colleague (yes, even your boss) know that you're a work in progress on this skill. That will help them manage their expectations of you, or encourage them to offer you some direction, or decide to bring their problem, challenge or opportunity to someone more skilled and seasoned—for now.

Deb remembers when her older brother Scott called her and asked, "Do you have any great team-building activities?" She responded (like the little sister she is), "Don't you know what I do for a living? Of course I have great team-building activities! How many do you want? Ten? Twenty? A hundred?"

Clearly, Scott accurately assessed that Deb would be able to help him in this area. For Deb, it was an opportunity to reciprocate for all of the parenting advice he'd given her over the years.

2. **Decide what you're willing to do.** Not only did Scott make a reasonable assumption that Deb *could* help him, he also intuited that she *would* help him. But this isn't always the case when someone asks you for help.

Think about your timing and capacity carefully and critically. Your friend may ask you to take some of her carpool shifts, but if it's going to make you late for work on those days, you may need to say no, or work out a different arrangement. Your boss may request that you onboard a new employee, and if that means you have less time to work on a time-sensitive client project, you may need to ask your boss to help you prioritize.

It's more than just finding time in your schedule. Helping others can take up headspace, too. Sure, it may not be a drain on your cognitive or emotional capacity to send your cousin a few suggestions for hotels for his upcoming trip to Singapore. But really listening to and empathizing with a friend who is going through a divorce (without you sharing your own experience or advice) can feel taxing.

You may also feel less confident about your own ability to deliver than the person asking you for help does about your abilities. For years, Deb's friends (and a few literary agents) have been suggesting that she write a parenting book. But while Deb has confidence in her ability to parent her *own* kids, she has less confidence that her approaches will help others. So, she keeps saying, "Thank you for asking me," and declining.

Finally, think about your motivation to help—honestly. As Dr. Esther Perel, author of *Mating in Captivity: Unlocking Erotic Intelligence*, and host of the "Where Shall We Begin" podcast, comments: "Sometimes when a person doesn't feel loved, they replace feeling loved with being needed." If your motivation to help someone is to feel loved, needed, important, seen, irreplaceable, etc., keep in mind that offering to help will likely not make those feelings go away. You may need to do some deeper work to get at the core of those drivers—with the help of a professional.

If your motivation to help someone is to avoid getting into trouble, to prevent emotional or physical threats, to dodge guilt or blame, etc., again, your act of help will only provide temporary relief. The cycle you're in is likely to continue, and again, may require some professional assistance to change.

But if your motivation is to contribute, make a positive impact, to fulfill a commitment you've entered into willingly, relieve someone's struggle, learn and grow yourself, advocate for an important cause, feel proud, and/or help someone else feel proud, go for it.

3. **Evaluate your relationship.** In his book *The Seven Habits of Highly Effective People*, author Stephen Covey uses the metaphor of an emotional bank account to describe the amount of trust that's been built up in a relationship.

Every relationship you have has an emotional and functional balance, made up of "deposits" and "withdrawals." A deposit is an action you take that puts trust into the relationship, while a withdrawal erodes trust.

Most healthy, long-term relationships have both de[and withdrawals. It's inevitable that each of you will do or say something that rubs the other person the wrong way, or disappoints them, or frustrates them. This could be showing up late, or forgetting to ask about their family, or cancelling meetings repeatedly. And, you'll both do things that light the other person up and make their life easier. This could be remembering their favorite snack (Deb and Sophie both agree on ice cream), or giving them helpful feedback, or taking something off their plate that's been stressful for them.

Think about this request for help in the context of your relationship bank account. Would your relationship benefit from an extra deposit right now to keep the emotional and functional balance in the black? Will making this deposit also feel good for you, too? If so, you might decide to say yes.

However, if making this deposit feels like a massive withdrawal to you—because it feels like you're being manipulated, gaslighted, or your own needs are being trampled—you may want to decline (if you can, safely). If your relationship is so far in the red that making this deposit will barely register (if at all), you may want to decline. And if it just feels wrong for your relationship right now, you may consider just saying no.

HOW TO SAY NO (WHEN SAYING NO IS AN OPTION).

As former UK Prime Minister Tony Blair remarked, "The art of leadership is saying no, not saying yes. It is very easy to say yes."

Saying no isn't easy for many of us—especially if we're habituated to say yes. For years, Deb had a sign in her office that said "Take a Day!" as a reminder to pause for 24 hours before saying yes to a request for her time (her family and closest friends were an exception to that rule).

You don't have to have a leadership title or position to wrestle with saying no. Regardless of role, responsibility, title, or position, you probably find yourself wanting to decline a request for your help, but you may not know how to say no assertively.

It's important to recognize the difference between a request and a command. A request is an ask for help to which we can say yes, no, or make a counteroffer. So, someone might ask you to brainstorm with them, and you might counter with: "I don't have the capacity to brainstorm with you right now, but once you have your list of ideas, I'd be happy to help you evaluate what you have. Would that work?"

A command assumes an obligation. However, you might think of requests as commands, sometimes due to the tone in which the request is made, or a power differential, or fear of the other person's reaction, or even a feeling of indebtedness. Let's face it: a request from your boss, or even your mother-in-law, can feel like a command even if saying no is, technically speaking, an option.

Nevertheless, while you know that "no" is a complete sentence when it comes to responding to a request for help, you might wrestle with being too passive (when you want to avoid conflict or hurt feelings), too aggressive (when you worry your needs will be ignored), or even passive-aggressive (when you're feeling manipulated, punished or otherwise concerned that an honest or direct approach won't work).

A passive approach to saying no might sound like "OK, I'll do it… this time" when you don't want to do it this time (or at all). Or it could sound like "Maybe I can" when you already know that you can't or don't want to say yes.

An aggressive reaction to a request for our help might range from asking "Can't you hear? I said no!" to "Not in a million years" or even "What makes you think I would want to do that?"

A passive-aggressive response can sound like "Fine" (when you're anything but). It can also sound like "Do I really have a choice?" It also shows up as "I'll get back to you" and you don't, or "Yeah, sure, I'll be there" and then you "forget" to show up.

As much as you don't want to disappoint, hurt or anger your friends, family, colleagues, clients, or others, you can be assertive and firm in your no's while being flexible enough to keep the door open for future yeses.

This requires you to be clear and honest about your own needs and preferences while honoring the needs and preferences of others (to be heard, to feel appreciated, to stay connected, to avoid embarrassment, to maintain their dignity in the face of rejection, etc.).

Here are several ways to say no assertively to a request for your help:

- I am so flattered that you asked but unfortunately, I can't.

- Normally, I would say yes to helping you with this, but I have already committed to_____.

- I need to say no, but I do hope you'll keep me in mind for the future.

- I cannot do that, but I wonder how I can help in some other way.

- Not this time, but thank you for thinking of me.

- I sit down with my calendar on Sundays. Would you please send me all of the information I need to make a decision, and I'll let you know on Monday if it works with my whole schedule?

- I can't make a decision right now about whether I can help you with this, and I don't want to hold you up, so feel free to ask someone else.

- I'm not available, but I know someone who could help. May I connect you?

- Thank you for asking me, and I know you asked me because you thought I'd be a good person to help with this. For the future, I want you to know that this isn't the kind of thing I'm likely to do. However, I would love to tell you the kind of help I tend to say yes to. Can I share that with you?

Keep in mind that anything you put into your own words will sound and feel more natural. But until you have your own words, these phrases are here for you to practice with.

HOW TO SAY NO (WHEN SAYING NO ISN'T AN OPTION).

There will be times when declining to help just isn't an option. Well, it may be an option, but it may not be the safe, smart, or strategic option. You *could* tell your boss that you can't help her roll out the new sales software, but since you're up for a promotion, it may not be the best time to decline. You *could* tell your son that you don't have the time to help him prepare for Friday's test, but since you've been trying to instill good study habits, you'd be undermining your own goals. Or, like Deb's friend Leslie shared with her one summer, she *could* say no to helping her elderly mother recover from heart surgery, or to her younger son as he finished his senior year of high school, or to her older son as he prepared to attend college in person after his first year online, or to her mother-in-law whose husband had recently passed away, or to her boss who needed her on a pressing legal case... but all of these were urgent and important, and required her time, energy, and attention. And so, she said yes.

Only *you* know whether saying no to a request for help will cause a bigger problem (short- or long-term) than agreeing to take this on—whatever it is. Use your judgment and take care of yourself if you find yourself needing to help more than feels comfortable to sustain over the long haul.

If this is the case for you, you may want to try some tiny but powerful acts of self-care to help you take care of yourself while taking care of others. Like what? Like:

- Step into the fresh air in the middle of the day.
- Listen to a playlist of your favorite songs.
- Take a walk, stretch, or do some form of exercise that doesn't feel like a chore to you.
- Discover a new podcast for entertainment, learning, or both.
- Treat yourself to a wonderful dessert.
- Make a charitable gift in any amount, to a cause that lights you up.
- Try to find a new favorite spot in your house—one that you've underestimated in the past.
- Call a friend or family member who always knows just how to pick you up, and who understands that you probably can only chat for three minutes, and that's totally fine.

- Wear something that makes you feel great about yourself.
- Pet an animal (but make sure it's one that *wants* to be petted).
- Thank someone who made a positive impact on you in a big or small way—and be detailed in your thanks.
- Burn a candle that smells divine to you.
- Refer to a mantra, saying or quotation that inspires you. Post it up somewhere you can see it when you need it.
- Breathe slowly.

Finally, consider external resources, both for the people who are asking you for help, and for yourself if you could use some support. This could include:

EAP (Employee Assistance Program)

Mental health professional

Medical doctor

Mentor

Coach

Spiritual/religious clergy, group, healer

Support group

Friends and family

Retreat

Addiction recovery specialist

Exercise instructor

Acupuncturist

Meditation expert

Financial planner

Accountant

Parenting expert

Gerontologist

Time management expert

Nutritionist

Massage therapist

Organizer

Pet care

Childcare

House cleaner

Personal care specialist (hair, nails, etc.)

You don't have to offer to help all the time, especially when it's not help that you can really give. Nor do you need to accept someone's request for help every time. It's not healthy or realistic. Once you start realizing that you can be helpful to others by saying yes when you *can* and *should*, and saying no when you're not the right person or it's not the right time, you'll free yourself to attend to what matters most.

CHAPTER 3: REVIEW AND REFLECT

REVIEW:

- Before offering help to others, or accepting requests for help, consider your skill and will on this particular task, and the quality of your relationship.

- You can say no assertively to many requests for help without damaging the relationship.

- When you can't say no to a request for help, practice self-care to help you build up your emotional and physical reserves.

REFLECT:

- Think about someone who has recently asked you for help. What did you consider in deciding to accept or decline the offer? And how do you feel about your decision?

- Consider a request for help you'd like to make. Who is most likely to have the skill and will to help with this task? And how would they (and you) describe your relationship?

CHAPTER 4:

YOU CAN'T HELP SOMEONE WHO DOESN'T WANT TO BE HELPED

As hard as it may be to ask for and accept help, it can be exponentially harder to try to help someone who doesn't want it.

You see your colleague struggling to design a client presentation. You offer to help her, especially since you've done dozens of these presentations already, and you have a template that could make her life *so* much easier, but she says, "No thank you. I really need to figure out how to do this on my own."

Your partner made a New Year's Resolution to take better care of his health. For the first six weeks of the year, he was going to sleep earlier so that he could get up for a daily walk. But now, he is back to staying up late to watch TV, and those walks are few and far between. You offer to help him get back on track, but he replies, "Don't bug me about this. I've got it handled."

When you see someone struggling with a problem or going about solving a problem the "wrong" way, your prosocial helping instinct likely kicks in. This is especially true if you have a stake in the outcome.

One of Deb's key findings as a parent and a coach is that the person who is most attached to a specific outcome has the most to lose. The more deeply and personally invested you are in your kid being the star pitcher on their baseball team (when they're on the fence between baseball and soccer), or in your spouse being skinny (when that's not a priority for them), or your boss exuding appreciation for your work (when they've never done that in the past), the more disappointed you will be when those outcomes don't materialize.

And so you're likely to "overstep" in your helping, which isn't helpful at all. In fact, your help is only truly helpful if the other person wants to be helped.

If you're like most people, you probably read that last sentence and thought, *Yeah, but...*

Yeah, but that doesn't apply to my kids.

Yeah, but my kind of help is different.

Yeah, but how else will I have it turn out the way I want it to?

Yeah, but if you give me the chance to help them, they'll realize they actually do want help.

This is when it's time to take a step back and think about why someone may not want your help, the consequences of helping someone who doesn't want to be helped, and what to do instead of helping.

THERE ARE VALID REASONS FOR NOT WANTING YOUR HELP.

When you wonder why someone doesn't want to accept your help (or any help), keep in mind that there are valid reasons why they are doing this. Even if you don't agree with their reasons, understanding why someone might refuse help can ease your frustration and make it easier for you to take a step back.

Try this: think about a time when someone offered to help you, and you said no. What were your reasons? (And even if you can't name them all, you probably had some—and they made perfect sense to you at the time!) Now think about what would have happened if that person had pushed and prodded you to take their help. Or maybe even refused to hear you, and stepped in and helped anyway. How would you feel about them? And how likely would you be to approach them for help in the future?

Probably not likely.

So, let's look at what _your_ reasons might have been, and apply them to our colleagues, friends, and family.

THEY CAN DO IT ON THEIR OWN/THEY DON'T NEED HELP.

There's a chance—and even a likelihood—that the person you are trying to help can actually handle their situation on their own. For example, when Sophie was applying to Duke University for college, she received offers from friends of friends to put in a good word for her with the admissions office. While Sophie appreciated this offer, she said no (and actually requested that they not say anything about her to the admissions office). While their outreach may have helped Sophie's chances of being admitted, Sophie felt strongly that she wanted to get in on her own merits. She didn't need someone's help to get into Duke and could handle the outcome (whether it be a rejection or admission) on her own.

(Good news! It was an admission!)

You may not know what the reason is that someone refuses your help, but with Sophie, she made it very clear that it had nothing to do with them personally and everything to do with herself and her own goals. She thanked them for their offers and told them that if she changed her mind, she would let them know. This kind of communication is not something you will always come across. Not everyone who refuses your help is going to thank you for your offer or explain their reasoning to you, but that's why you need to keep in mind that there are real reasons for not wanting help.

THEY HAD A BAD PAST EXPERIENCE WITH RECEIVING HELP.

When Deb facilitates public speaking workshops for her corporate clients, the primary challenge she faces isn't helping these leaders manage their performance anxiety or figure out what to do with their hands. Her biggest challenge is that most of these professionals have experienced presentation skills training in the past, and found it unhelpful. Some of them had worked with an instructor who tried to make them sound like someone else. Others had remembered feeling deeply embarrassed in front of a group of their peers. And still others felt like they forgot everything they'd learned, so they weren't convinced that this time would be any different.

As a result, those who opt-in to Deb's workshops are usually those who have had a positive experience with being helped in the past, and therefore are bringing some degree of skill and will to the program. Those who need help the most, however, rarely get it because their past exposure to this kind of help was so disappointing.

Deb has also been on the other side of this equation. Growing up as an overweight child, Deb's pediatrician "fat shamed" her at every annual checkup. While his intention may have been to help her create healthier habits around food and exercise, his impact was so unhelpful that it led Deb to a lifelong fear of going to the doctor. She wasn't as worried about getting a painful injection or a frightening diagnosis as she was about feeling bad, embarrassed, ashamed, or unworthy.

It is only in recent years that Deb has started to advocate for what she wants and needs at the doctor. What does this look like? When the nurse or physician's assistant asks her to hop on the scale, she says, "No thank you. I'm skipping it for my mental health."

(And she hasn't gotten into an argument yet!)

If the person you're trying to help has a bad taste in their mouth from previous attempts to help them that undermined their self-esteem, or pointed them in a direction they didn't want to go, then you'll likely face help-resistance.

THEY SEE HELP THROUGH A DIFFERENT CULTURAL LENS THAN YOU DO.

Asking for and receiving help can mean so many different things to different people.

It could mean: "I am a part of a family, and helping is what family members do for one another."

And it could also mean: "I am a part of a family, and asking for help might bring shame or embarrassment to my family."

It could mean: "This is how you get better at your job."

And it could also mean: "This is how people find out you don't know how to do your job."

How, when, where, and by whom you were raised impacts your help-seeking mindsets and behaviors—as these factors do for everyone around you.

The person you want to help may have fundamentally different beliefs, norms and values about help than you have. These have a direct impact on whether someone believes that they are in need of help, whether or not they seek help, from whom, what kind, and how forthcoming they are about help in general.

For example, collectivistic cultures, such as those in China, Korea, Japan, Costa Rica, and Indonesia, emphasize interdependence and social harmony within the group. As a result, people who were raised in these cultures may put what's good for the group above personal interests and motives. In comparison, cultures that are more individualistic, such as The United States, Australia, New Zealand, Canada, and The United Kingdom, tend to put personal motives over group values.

So you might notice that your colleague in Beijing is less likely to seek (or even accept) help outside his own team, while your colleague in Brisbane is more apt to say, "Thanks for the offer—I'll take the help!"

Of course, that's not always the case. And there are myriad factors that impact one's culture, beliefs, practices, and values when it comes to accepting help. For example, if your husband's parents embarrassed him when he asked for help at age eight, it's possible that asking for and accepting help may be hard for him at age 58. If your direct report has always kept her problems to herself and values privacy, then don't take it personally when she doesn't want to confide in you—even if you really, truly mean to help.

And rather than try to figure out the cultural nuances of every person you work with or play with, ask yourself this question:

"What don't I understand about this person that may contribute to their thoughts, feelings, and actions around accepting help?"

(Assume it's a lot.)

THEY WANT THE OPPORTUNITY TO GROW AND LEARN THROUGH MISTAKES.

When you help someone, you are often trying to help them avoid mistakes or mitigate losses. Maybe you are helping them solve a small parenting challenge now so it doesn't become an unmanageable parenting challenge down the road. Or you're giving them advice for the first 90 days in a new role to increase their chances of having a successful start to their job.

Often, though, making mistakes and recovering from a loss is a major part of how people learn to be successful. If you are constantly helping someone, it's hard for them to grow and learn.

During her sophomore year at Duke, Sophie's thrifting resale business started to grow. She excitedly told her parents about the sales she had made, the hundred-dollar T-shirt she had found for $1.29, and her plans to post her items across multiple platforms so that her business could grow. Deb offered to help Sophie by posting about her business on Facebook, where Deb had thousands of followers who could and would promote Sophie's online store. While this was a genuine offer, Sophie told her mom that she wanted to see if her business was successful without anyone's help. If her mom posted about it on Facebook, Sophie wouldn't know whether she was successful because of her own work or because of her mom's network. In addition, Sophie wanted the opportunity to fail. If someone was always there to buy her products, how would she know which products the market really wanted, and which ones weren't worth her time and money?

Ask yourself this: What is a skill or behavior you learned through trial and error—and that you're glad you did?

THEIR SELF-ESTEEM IS GETTING IN THE WAY OF THEM ACCEPTING HELP.

Many of us believe that if we ask for help, it means we're unskilled, incompetent, or unsuccessful. You may have thought to yourself:

If I accept help, it's proof I can't do it on my own.

I'm the boss. I can't accept help from my employees.

What can these Gen-Z kids teach me that I don't already know?

These are just some of the mindsets that someone who is reluctant to ask for or accept help may be wrestling with.

When Sophie started her position as a teacher's assistant for a statistics course at Duke, she was a first-year student. All of the students who she was teaching were second-, third-, and fourth-year students. As soon as those students found out how old Sophie was, many of them were reluctant to receive help from her. Their belief that someone younger shouldn't be helping someone older was getting in the way of Sophie doing her job, which was to help them with statistics. While this was a temporary problem (many were struggling so much that they conceded and accepted Sophie's help), this is not an uncommon one.

IT'S YOU.

The hard truth is that they may not want your help because it's coming from *you*. While the classic line is "it's not you, it's me," in this case, it might actually be you.

How so?

- Perhaps you've offered help in the past that wasn't actually helpful.

- Perhaps you've said, "I told you so" when someone didn't take your help.

- Perhaps you expected to be thanked over and over again.

- Perhaps you think you are more of an expert than the other person thinks you are.

- Perhaps your experience isn't as relevant as you think it is.

- Perhaps you say you're helping but you totally take over.

- Perhaps your help comes with strings attached.

- Perhaps you expressed that the other person shouldn't need help.

- Perhaps you can't offer the help they need.

- Perhaps you didn't demonstrate empathy about their struggle.

- Perhaps you didn't keep their prior ask for help confidential.

And, if you're looking at this list and thinking to yourself, *Nope, not me!* try two things:

First, apply the "2% True Rule." In other words, ask yourself, "If I had to admit that I may be the reason someone doesn't want my help, what 2% of that would be true?" (For Deb, it is at least 2% true that she can take over if she has expertise in the area of help;

for Sophie, it is at least 2% true that she might not demonstrate empathy if it's a problem she thinks you could have avoided.)

Second, ask the other person, "How do I make it hard for you to ask me for help?" And then, stop talking, really listen, don't defend or justify your approach, and commit to getting better. (Not sure how to get better? Ask a colleague, friend, or family member for help!)

IT'S PAINFUL NOT TO HELP.

We don't like to see others struggle, especially when we care about them, and truly believe that we can make things easier for them. If you see an elderly person crossing the street, and they insist that they can do it themselves (despite moving so slowly that they risk not crossing before the light turns red), it is difficult to stand there and watch. It can be even more challenging to step back when you have the resources available to help someone.

When you're not sure what kind of help someone needs, or whether or not you even have something meaningful to offer, you are less likely to feel torn about offering help. However, when you have the capacity, experience, time, energy, money, or connections that might make someone's experience easier, but they don't want your help, you may find yourself struggling to back off.

When Jake was in high school, he was involved in both History Bowl and theater. When he competed at the National History Bee and Bowl three years in a row, Deb was there to cheer him on, but her lack of historical knowledge meant that she couldn't offer him help beyond that. So she wasn't even tempted to try. As it turns out, he was just fine on his own, coming in 5th place in the nation.

His theater performances were a different story. Deb had performed in plays, sung in choirs, done improvisational, sketch, and stand-up comedy throughout her childhood through her 20's. She knew that she had the background and experience to help Jake hone his craft.

But you know what Jake didn't want? Help from his mom. So Deb bit her tongue and backed off. And it was *hard*.

While Deb wanted Jake to steal the show, at the end of the day, she also knew that however well he performed on stage wasn't really going to impact her. However, it's particularly challenging to not help when you are attached to a particular outcome. Let's say that you and your coworker are collaborating on a sales plan to present to your manager. You've done your part, and your colleague is working on theirs. You only have a week to complete the project and, with only one day left, your coworker has not completed their deliverables. Why do you want to step in and help? Because you care about the outcome regardless of how much you care about your coworker.

And let's say you really *do* care about your coworker. Then you have an additional reason to want to help, because you're attached to both the project outcome and the interpersonal outcome.

Try this: Think about someone you feel close to. Imagine they are applying for a new job and you know that they haven't updated their resume since college. Now imagine that they have expressed that they do not want any help in the application process, but you know that their disorganized resume will likely be the reason why they don't even get an interview. They've been clear they don't want help. You know you both care about them and have the resources to help them. What do you do?

Maybe you've decided that if they say they don't want help, it means you shouldn't help, even if you know you can. Or maybe you decided that you would try talking to them just one more time. Or emailing them a copy of your resume so that they have a good model to follow. Or texting them the name of a resume-writing consultant. If you chose anything other than the first option, you should understand the consequences of helping someone who doesn't want to be helped.

In other words, you *can* try to help someone who doesn't want it, but don't expect to be rewarded for your good intentions.

WHEN YOU "HELP" SOMEONE WHO DOESN'T WANT YOUR HELP.

Your offer to help is genuine. You don't mean to embarrass anyone or contribute to them feeling helpless, useless or less-than. You know what you have to offer can make a difference for them. The only problem is they don't feel the same way.

You may want to cover your son's rent when he's trying to establish himself as financially independent.

You may want to take a tricky client conversation off your direct report's plate when she wants to learn how to navigate these conflicts for herself.

You may want to introduce your friend to a few single folks when it is clear that he isn't ready to date again (even though you think he's overdue to "get back out there").

It's possible that if you try to help someone who doesn't want help, you will push them away—if they haven't already pushed you away first.

Chances are, at some point you've thought to yourself something like this: *I don't understand why they won't just accept my help!*

Now get honest with yourself—really honest. Do you mean "I don't understand why…" or do you *really* mean "I don't like that…?"

You probably *do* understand why they don't want help. In fact, if you were in their shoes you might be making the same decision that they are making now.

So you say, "I don't understand why they won't accept my help" instead of "I don't like that they won't accept my help," because not understanding something is a lot easier to deal with emotionally than not liking something (and not being able to change it).

Frustration is likely to set in if you don't like what someone else is deciding to do. And when you do feel frustrated, you might act out or withdraw. This might look like one or more of these behaviors:

Sulking

Blaming

Defending yourself

Shutting down

Walking away

Criticizing

Yelling

Manipulating

Threatening

Talking behind someone's back

Self-soothing with food, drugs, alcohol, overwork, sleeping, etc.

Do any of those look familiar? If so, know that you're not alone in having a hard time when someone ignores or blocks your attempts to help. And also know that naming this source of stress aloud can be the first step toward reducing your reaction. Say to yourself or to a trusted friend, colleague, or family member, "I notice that I am feeling hurt that Lily doesn't want my advice" or "I recognize that I am frustrated that Sam doesn't want me to get involved."

And then... stop. Don't spiral into a story. Don't justify why you are in the right and they are in the wrong. Don't try to drum up support for your thwarted attempts. Just sit with your discomfort, give yourself credit for your prosocial intentions, pat yourself on the back for putting the other person's preferences ahead of your own, and trust that you will survive this challenging experience.

Yes, your discomfort may be tough to tolerate. But keep in mind that when you help where your help is not wanted, your friend or colleague may interpret that as you not trusting them. And that's a bitter pill for them to swallow.

Imagine you are an engineer. You are working on a project to create a blueprint of a new school your company is building. You know you can do this successfully, as you have done this many times over the past two decades, but your colleague keeps peeking over your shoulder and offering to help you. How would this make you feel? You'd probably feel like your colleague doesn't trust you to do the work. And then you may even start questioning your own abilities. That's not a good feeling.

If you're the colleague, your intentions aren't to make someone else feel untrustworthy, but that's the impact. And the impact is what we want to focus on when improving our help-offering skills. Otherwise, we don't just lose this opportunity to help; we risk future opportunities to offer help when the time is right.

WHAT TO DO WHEN YOUR HELP ISN'T WANTED.

You may already understand why the person you're trying to help doesn't want help. But if you don't, take a moment to think about why they aren't accepting help. Challenge yourself to think about it from their perspective, rather than yours.

For example, let's say that your aging mother, who has been cooking her own food for years, has started to have some minor accidents in the kitchen. Of course, you want to help, but she refuses your help. Why might that be?

Maybe she is in denial about her age and physical abilities.

Maybe she doesn't want to burden you.

Maybe she does want help, but from a friend rather than her child.

There are plenty of reasons why she might not accept help, and it's important that you allow yourself to think beyond the "she's just stubborn" or "she just doesn't realize she needs my help" mentality.

Also, if you assess your relationship with that person and feel comfortable, you can gently ask them why they don't want to accept help. Research shows that perspective-getting (asking someone to share their perspective) is more accurate than perspective-taking (you trying to imagine their perspective). You might learn that they don't want help from you, but would accept it from an expert in their field. Or that the kind of help you're offering just isn't what they need right now. Which leads to the next thing you can do: increase your help fluency.

If you notice that your offers of help are being rebuffed, you may want to consider whether your offers are limited in their range and effectiveness. Perhaps you're a fix-it kind of person. Maybe you're really good at listening without judgment or brainstorming ideas. While it's possible that the person you're trying to help doesn't want help, it may also be the case that they don't want or need the one or two types of help on your menu.

It's time to expand your services!

Your kid might not want you to correct their grammar in their speech or help brainstorm ideas for what else they can say. And you might think that they just don't want help. But maybe they would prefer for you to give them a pep talk or cheerlead. Maybe they want help celebrating after they finish writing the speech. Or maybe they just want you to sit next to them, and you do your work silently while they do theirs.

There's no quick and easy way to become help fluent. It takes time. It takes reading this book (feel free to skip to Part 2 if you can't wait another moment) and practicing the mindset shifts and exercises in it. It takes patience, intention, practice, and feedback. But you are already on the right track, and have taken the first step just by reading this book.

Finally, while it may be frustrating not to be able to help your colleague, friend, or family member, you can use that energy on someone else.

Your kid doesn't want help with their term paper for their English class? Offer to help your struggling coworker on a proposal. Your coworker doesn't want help? Volunteer by visiting residents at a nursing home, or sorting canned goods at a food bank, or raise money for a philanthropic organization whose cause is meaningful to you. Your help will be welcomed, appreciated, and go a long way in all of these places.

REMOVE "I TOLD YOU SO" FROM YOUR VOCABULARY.

When someone refuses your help, and, as it turns out, really could have benefitted from it, you might be tempted to say "I told you so."

"I told you your boss wouldn't want your feedback on his presentation."

"I told you not to eat a burger before going on the boat."

"I told you that going behind your colleague's back wasn't a good idea."

Few phrases make people bristle as much as "I told you so." First of all, when someone has made a misstep or an error in judgment, they certainly don't want to be reminded of it. This can lead the person you were hoping to help feel shame, which, according to research, can make them feel exposed, vulnerable, and angry. It's embarrassing and belittling, neither of which create healthy working or living relationships.

Second of all, saying "I told you so" can be interpreted as a way of you seeking credit for your intelligence or foresight—which is fine, except when it's clearly at the expense of their project, their dignity, or your relationship.

Third, it's often an indirect or passive-aggressive way of expressing hurt that your colleague or friend didn't accept your help, frustration that they ignored their counsel, or even anger that they picked a different approach from what you would have done or suggested.

What makes hearing "I told you so" additionally irritating and unnecessary? Our hindsight bias (also known as the "knew-it-all-along effect") where, after something has already happened, our natural inclination kicks in to see that event as having been predictable—whether or not we actually predicted it. In other words, the person who didn't take your help is already telling themselves "I told *me* so" without needing to hear it from you.

Hearing "I told you so" has never helped anyone feel better or do better, so don't say it. Better yet, get rid of your *future* "I told you so's" now so that if it turns out you were right, you can be supportive instead of condescending.

TALK TO A PROFESSIONAL.

Professionals, like therapists or coaches, don't only work with those who have mental illnesses or those who are struggling to function. Everyone, including you, deserves to have a safe place to talk openly about their frustrations, fears, and concerns. In fact, if you are trying to help someone who doesn't want help, you are likely feeling frustrated and worried, so there's no one better to talk to than a professional, even if it's just to let out your anger so that you don't let it out on someone else (like your spouse or your boss).

It can be hard to see the people around us struggle when we believe that we can help them. It's also a challenge to understand how to back off when someone says they don't want help. But now you also know what you can do instead so you don't waste your time or energy on someone who doesn't want it or welcome it. And, more importantly, so that you don't damage your relationship in the process.

THERE ARE EXCEPTIONS FOR WHEN YOU SHOULD HELP SOMEONE WHO DOESN'T WANT HELP.

Just like any other rule, there are exceptions. Sometimes (but not as often as you may think or wish), you need to step in and help someone even when the other person absolutely, positively, doesn't want it.

Because it is hard to know when you *think* you should break the rule as opposed to when you should actually break it, here are some scenarios to consider.

WHEN SOMEONE IS AT RISK OF SIGNIFICANT AND/ OR IRREPARABLE HARM.

If the person you are trying to help refuses help, but they are at risk of self-harming, dying by suicide, or hurting someone else, you help them, even if that means putting your relationship at stake. When Sophie speaks to middle and high schoolers, they often ask her what to do if their friends tell them that they want to kill themselves. Sophie always tells them that their friend's life is more important than their friendship, and their friendship can't be continued if the friend is dead. Keep this in mind when someone says they don't want help. If they are in this kind of situation, you step in and help, always.

Loss of life isn't the only significant harm where you may want to step in. If you see someone behaving in a way that puts them, their family, colleagues, or company at risk for reputational, legal and/ or financial harm, go for it.

For example, if you hear someone make a homophobic, racist, or sexist remark, that can put them at reputational risk, and—if it's in the workplace—can put your company in legal or financial jeopardy. You should either step in to help them stop this behavior, or find someone in a more appropriate position to do so.

And this is a good reminder that helping another person doesn't always require *you* to be the helper. You may not have the expertise, relationship, power, influence, time, etc. to help, but that doesn't mean that you shouldn't get involved. According to Jewish tradition shared in Pirkei Avot (*The Ethics of Our Fathers*): "You need not complete the work, but you are not free to desist from it."

WHEN THEY HAVE DIMINISHED CAPACITY.

If the person you are trying to help has diminished emotional, cognitive, or intellectual capacity, you may want to assert yourself more than you otherwise would.

When Deb's mother-in-law (Sophie's grandmother), Joan, passed away from lung cancer in 2018, Deb's father-in-law Archie was clearly suffering. He and Joan hadn't been separated for more than ten days in their 52-year marriage, and he was in shock at her sudden death.

And yet, none of his children asked him if he needed help. Why? Because they knew that he did need help and they also knew that, if asked, he would say no.

So they all just helped, assertively, insistently, and immediately. From writing thank you notes and taking over the bookkeeping to stocking his freezer with single-serve meals and visiting him daily, his family surrounded him with support, direction, and love.

It's important to note that when someone is feeling sad, scared, or hopeless, you do not have carte blanche to step in and take over for them. In fact, that kind of help can feel minimizing and patronizing. But when someone is experiencing the kind of grief where they aren't exactly sure what to do next, and every single decision feels paralyzing, you might want to help by taking that next step together.

This isn't just an emotional issue. If someone in your life has diminished cognitive or intellectual capacity, it is likely your role to step in and help. This does *not* mean your colleague whom you think is an "idiot." This does refer to your aging parent who has dementia, or your child who has significant learning delays.

And even then, if there's something your dad or daughter thinks they can do without you, and there is low risk of harm (financial, legal, physical, etc.), you may want to let them try it.

WHEN IT IS YOUR JOB TO HELP THEM.

If it is your job to help someone, then you help them whether they want it or not. If you are a firefighter, it doesn't matter whether the person in the burning building wants you to help them out. You do it anyway.

When you have a job that is not an occupation (like being a parent), it can be harder to figure out when it is actually your job to help someone. For parents, it really comes down to ages and stages of the child. For example, it is not your job to help your adult child (who should be able to self-regulate emotions, and of course there are exceptions) get through a meltdown when they don't want your help. However, if your ten-year-old is having a meltdown or a tantrum, it is your job to help them because they might not have the ability to regulate and control their own emotions.

When Deb started teaching at Wharton Business School, she took Sophie to the UPenn bookstore to buy a shirt. If you know Sophie at all, you know she takes her swag very seriously. After 30 minutes in the bookstore, Sophie began to cry. She could not decide which shirt she wanted and was having a meltdown. Sure, part of this was probably because she was hungry, but nonetheless, it was Deb's job to say, "Stop. It's time to go." Because Sophie had diminished emotional capacity at that time, and because she was young enough that she was not able to handle her emotions on her own, it was Deb's job as a parent to step in and help, whether or not Sophie wanted help.

WHEN YOU UNDERSTAND THAT THEY DON'T WANT YOUR HELP, AND YOU ARE PREPARED TO ACCEPT THE CONSEQUENCES OF HELPING ANYWAY.

You're going to have to do a cost-benefit analysis for each situation.

If you decide to help your 23-year-old son with his household expenses after he told you that he wants to try to support himself, you may benefit by feeling less worried. What could it cost? His sense of independence and autonomy, and interpersonal trust in your relationships.

When Deb went to coaching school, she was cautioned repeatedly by her seasoned instructors not to coach her family members. When Deb arrived home from coaching school, she was so eager to put her new skills into action that she immediately coached Michael (who, as her husband, is very much a family member) on a career challenge. The benefit? Deb got to try out her coaching skills ASAP. The cost? The biggest argument they've had in more than two decades of marriage. (I guess those coaching teachers knew a few things, huh?)

Yes, you can try to help someone who doesn't want it. But recognize that it probably won't turn out as you'd like it to, in the short term *and* the long term.

Instead, think about someone who really, truly wants the help that you can and want to give—and gift it to them. You'll both be glad you did.

CHAPTER 4: REVIEW AND REFLECT

 REVIEW:

- You cannot help someone who doesn't want your help—as painful and frustrating as it may be.

- Someone may not want your help for a variety of reasons, including their cultural norms, their sense of autonomy, their commitment to their own development, or because it's you.

- When someone is at high risk—emotionally, physically, financially, legally, reputationally—you may have to step in to help, even if they are protesting your involvement.

REFLECT:

- Who is someone you've been trying to help who doesn't seem to want it? How is your persistence impacting your relationship? What are some alternative approaches?

- Who keeps trying to help you, despite you rebuffing their attempts? What is it about them or the help they're offering that has you saying no? What, if anything, could they do differently that *would* be helpful? And, if there's nothing, how might you be more assertive that you don't want their assistance?

CHAPTER 5:

YOU DON'T NEED TO DO IT ALL YOURSELF (AND YOU SHOULDN'T)

We've all seen the headlines:

"How to get more done in less time!"

"How to get more hours out of your day!"

"Work smarter, not harder!"

And chances are, you've clicked on one or two… or ten, just like that.

Most of us find ourselves in a pickle: we want to get more done *and* we recognize that we can't do it all. But recognizing that dilemma and doing something about it are two different things.

So, before we can make a change to get better at asking for and accepting help, let's start by acknowledging that trying to do it all *ourselves* is a mistake—one with serious ramifications to our physical, mental, emotional, reputational, and interpersonal wellbeing.

OUR BODIES ARE TAXED BY OVERWORK.

According to the National Safety Council's statistics, around 4.6 million workplace injuries happen across the US every year, and risk grows when people work overtime. And injuries aren't the only physical impact.

A 2017 study of over 85,000 working adults that spanned an entire decade showed that people who work more than 55 hours a week puts them at a heightened risk of obesity, alcohol consumption, smoking addiction, back pain, stroke, diabetes, and cardiac disease.

And that's just the risks associated with overwork *at work.* Add childcare responsibilities, caring for aging parents, involvement in community or volunteer organizations, etc., and the physical toll can be even greater.

OUR MENTAL HEALTH IS AT RISK.

In their Harvard Business Review article *"An Early Warning System for Your Team's Stress Level,"* INSEAD professors Thomas Hellwig, Caroline Rook, Elizabeth Florent-Treacy, and Manfred F. R. Kets de Vries share that our mental performance is impacted by stress (and trying to do it all ourselves is indeed a stressor). Under stress, we have trouble concentrating, collaborating, making decisions, problem-solving, and thinking rationally.

This becomes a vicious cycle. In order to get things accomplished, we need to be able to concentrate, collaborate, make decisions, solve problems, and think rationally. And yet, the more we push ourselves, the less cognitive capacity we have for those critical executive functions.

DOING IT ALL TAKES AN EMOTIONAL TOLL.

Deb is not a frequent crier. Her weepy episodes tend to be limited to re-watching the 1983 Academy Award-winning movie *Terms of Endearment,* banging her little toe on the coffee table, and finding herself with too much to do and not enough emotional resources to get it all done. This typically occurs when Deb is facing multiple client deadlines at once, or when she has a work obligation that competes with a family obligation—and feels like she doesn't have ideal options for getting this handled.

Under the stress of trying to do it all without asking for and accepting help, many of us experience a loss of emotional control. For some, this may show up as being irritable (or being more irritable than usual for them), or having an uncharacteristic outburst, withdrawing, or, in Deb's case, crying.

Research from the academic journal *Work & Stress* highlights one type of task in particular that can contribute significantly to feelings of depression and anxiety—and you probably have this kind of task on your plate. What is it? These are tasks which you see as "illegitimate."

An illegitimate task is one where you think to yourself, *I shouldn't have to do this* because it's unreasonable *(it falls outside of the range of my role)* and/or it's unnecessary *(there has to be a better/simpler/more efficient way; this could have been prevented; or I'm not sure what purpose this serves).*

The more you think to yourself *I shouldn't have to do this,* the more likely you are to feel anxious, depressed, and full of despair. But there's good news: the more you think to yourself *I shouldn't have to do this all by myself,* the better off you will be!)

WE PUT OUR REPUTATIONS AT RISK.

When Deb was a child, her parents often told her: "You're very resourceful. You'll figure it out." It was intended to be a compliment, reinforcing their belief in her tenacity, perseverance, and creativity. How Deb *heard* it, however, was different from its intended impact. She interpreted this as "You're very resourceful. You'll figure it out *yourself.*"

Over time, Deb came to believe that she was expected to figure out how to do *everything* herself—work, parenting, marriage, friendship, health, finances, etc.—and assumed there would be a reputational cost to asking for help.

What might people think if she needed help? Maybe they'd think that she was incompetent, unintelligent, lazy... and the list went on.

Sound familiar? You might fear that asking for help will make you look bad. And ironically, the opposite is often true. When you believe that you have to do it all, you put yourself (and your colleagues and families) at risk for making *a reputation-ruining mistake.*

Think about it. You are much more likely to turn in sub-par work, deliver partial or incomplete results, and make mistakes when you are stressed and overwhelmed. And those mistakes can cost you time, money, energy, resources, and yes—your credibility as well.

THERE ARE INTERPERSONAL COSTS OF DOING IT ALONE.

When you assume you have to do it all yourself, you run the risk of cutting off your friends, family, colleagues, networks, and others who can and want to help you.

The best-case scenario if you don't ask for help is that people will assume you don't need help—and will move on to offering help to others who want it and welcome it. The worst case is that people consider you uncollaborative, isolated, unapproachable, lacking self-awareness, not a team player, self-oriented, and not growth-oriented (and then you'll probably need help repairing your relationships).

There are additional interpersonal costs. When you don't ask others for help, they may feel like they can't ask *you* for help, either. You also don't learn from others' expertise and experience. Furthermore, you miss the opportunity to connect and build rapport with people who may have experienced the same challenges or dilemmas you face. Finding out you're not alone in your struggles can feel like a huge relief—and you won't have the chance to experience that, or let someone else experience it, too.

Finally, research shows that your mental wellbeing impacts the mental wellbeing of your colleagues and your family, too. Your stress is contagious. Is that what you want to pass around—and pass along?

And just in case the physical, mental, emotional, reputational, and interpersonal costs of trying to do it all yourself aren't enough, there are additional challenges to be aware of.

Trying to do it all yourself is absolutely unrealistic.

Have you seen this phrase that keeps circling the internet? "You have the same number of hours in the day as Beyoncé."

Yes, in *theory*, we all have the same 24 hours in a day. In reality, some of us have more autonomy about how we spend it than others. Some of us have different priorities about how we spend our time than others. And, most importantly when it comes to Beyoncé, some of us have more help than others. While Beyoncé didn't respond to the authors' request to be interviewed for this book, Deb and Sophie can surmise that her team includes everyone from hairdressers, makeup artists, and stylists to drivers, publicists, and a team of lawyers—all of whom give her more freedom to choose how she spends her time and energy.

So, stop comparing yourself *to* Beyoncé (or to anyone else, for that matter) and start borrowing *from* Beyoncé. Borrow what? Her diamonds? Her gowns? Her jet? If she'll lend those to you, great. But if not, you can still borrow her mindset that you can't do it all yourself. We all need help. Even Queen B.

To be clear, this isn't a Beyoncé problem. Unrealistic expectations about how much any one of us can do ourselves without help from others is a larger issue. Technology has made an "always on" culture the norm, which contributes to us feeling like we can and should be available to produce and perform all the time. This takes a toll on our health. Researchers at the University of California, Irvine found that the heart rates of employees with constant access to office email stayed in a perpetual "high alert" mode. Those without constant email access were less stressed.

And if your answer to this challenge is "multitasking," think again. Research shows that multitasking does not work for 97.5% of people. (So yes, that probably means you!) Trying to do two activities at once impairs your best thinking, divides your attention, slows your learning, and prevents you from completing tasks effectively. Which means that you end up with more to do, not less.

OUR BRAINS ARE CONSPIRING AGAINST US.

When you feel like you are expected to do it all without help, your confirmation bias trains your brain to see proof of this everywhere: your email chime is "proof" that you need to get back to work; your phone ringing is "proof" that your friend needs your advice right now; your kid asking "what's for dinner?" is "proof" that you need to plan and prepare tonight's balanced menu before the family gets hangry; your stack of bills is "proof" that you need to take care of the family finances ASAP; and so on. For as long as you believe that it's all up to you, you will easily find evidence to support it.

And for as long as you feel like you have to do it all *yourself*, you will also see these cues and clues everywhere to support this belief. You'll notice that the client follow-up calls you delegated to your direct report were done mostly right—but not 100% right. Wouldn't it have just been better for you to have done it yourself? You'll observe that the wet towels you asked your teenager to pick up from the bathroom floor are still there, growing more mildewed by the minute. Shouldn't you just have done a big scoop up while you were in there anyway? The more you do it yourself, the more you'll see the signs that doing it yourself is the *best* or *only* way. You'll quickly find yourself in a vicious cycle that leaves you exhausted—and alone.

It also leaves you and others stagnating. By taking back the "almost but not quite right" client calls from your direct report, you'll stay stuck doing them, and she won't develop her skills. By picking up the towels from the bathroom floor, you'll be doing all the laundry all the time, and your teen will have been rewarded for ignoring your request. None of us grow by doing what we've always done—and that includes you.

Deb's client Tan was committed to diversity recruitment and hiring for his business unit in a Fortune 100 firm. He shared his vision, goals, and metrics for this challenge with his team leads, with the intention of having them take accountability and ownership for increasing the number and quality of diverse candidates they sourced. Tan gave them a year to meet these metrics, and then confessed to Deb in a coaching session, "I hope they can rise to the challenge, but I'm not optimistic."

Deb explored that mindset with Tan, and shared with him the research that correlates our expectations of others with their actual performance. Tan's belief that his team wouldn't ultimately deliver would likely have an impact on their goal achievement—or lack thereof. And yet, Tan's confirmation bias was so unshakeable that within four months of sharing his ambitious diversity goals, he took the initiative back from his team leads. He decided to just do it all himself. As a result, five preventable things happened: First, he had to put other important work on the back burner so that he could dedicate his time to diversity recruitment; second, Tan was already overburdened when his manager asked him to consider taking on a new, exciting project that was aligned with their new CEO's vision for the company, and had to decline this opportunity; third, his team leads felt like he didn't trust them (which he didn't) and this had a negative impact on the morale of his group; fourth, Tan had to do all of the diversity work himself; and fifth, since he was doing it all by himself, he didn't meet his goals.

Talk about a lose-lose.

Let's face it: there will always be more to do. There will always be someone who can do, but just may not do it the same way *you* would do it. There will always be opportunities to confirm your belief that you should just do it all, or do it yourself, so that you won't be disappointed.

And there will also be other opportunities to try a different mindset, a new approach, and decide to ask for help so that you don't have to do it all yourself.

Like right now.

So let's start with the right mindset. Or *mindsets* as the case may be.

As mentioned earlier, a mindset is a set of beliefs, perspectives, or attitudes you hold that drive the way you handle situations, how you think about what is going on, and what you should do.

We've already briefly discussed a **Growth Mindset**—the belief that we are still learning and growing, and that we can recover from setbacks.

Let's look at a second mindset, the **Resourceful Mindset**.

In order for you to create the space and willingness to ask for and accept help from others, you need to believe that you are resourceful. In other words, if you trust that you have resources that you can tap into, then you're more likely to give yourself the time and space for that to happen. You're also less likely to believe that you can only have help in an emergency, or that you need to be rescued, or that you only have one resource you can count on.

A resourceful mindset can sound like this:

"I know that there are lots of people who can help me."

"I believe that there are lots of people who want to help me."

"I know that if one of my resources isn't available, I have others I can turn to."

"I know that I don't have to wait until I'm desperate or in crisis to reach out to my network for help."

Which one of these mindsets are you willing to try today?

A third mindset is an **Appreciative Mindset**—one that Deb uses a lot with her clients. This draws from Dr. David Cooperrider's work on Appreciative Inquiry, which is the process of getting curious (the inquiry part) about what's working when it's working well in order to grow it (the appreciative part).

So how do we bring an appreciative mindset to our conversations with ourselves about asking for help? By remembering that we have many things in our life that are going well, as well as areas where we could use some help. By being grateful for our colleagues, friends, family, and outside experts who can and will assist us. By recalling past times when we asked others for help—and it was exactly what we needed.

Try this: remember a time when you asked someone for help and it had exactly the positive impact you were hoping for. What mindset did you bring to asking for help? Who did you ask? How did you ask? What are you proud of? What made this experience such a valuable one for you?

This leads to a fourth mindset: a **Hopeful Mindset.** Paula Davis, Founder of the Stress & Resilience Institute, and author of *Beating Burnout at Work: Why Teams Hold the Secret to Well-Being and Resilience,* writes about the four core beliefs of this mindset, and Sophie and Deb have added their perspective in italics:

"Hopeful people share four core beliefs:

1. That their future will be better than their present—*and asking for help can make this easier and more fulfilling;*

2. That they have the power to direct how their lives unfold—*and you can ask for help while still directing your life;*

3. That there are many paths to their goals—*and most of us will need help along some of those paths;*

4. That there will be obstacles **and** that they can overcome them—*with help.*"

Finally, here's one mindset to avoid: "I deserve help." Yes, you probably *do* deserve it, but trying to decide between what you do and don't deserve can lead to feelings of guilt, and create a sense of scarcity. As Dr. Esther Perel comments: "'Deserving' is the entitlement of the deprived. Deprived people don't just say, 'I want something, it's OK.' They need to 'deserve' it to muster the energy to allow themselves to do it. It becomes a dialogue with the deprivation: 'How much have I given of myself to now feel like it's OK to give this to myself?' It's a complete economic system."

If you feel like you need to "muster the energy" to allow yourself help, then you're not truly bought into the idea that you can and should have help. Yes, you. Yes, right now. And yes, even if you're not feeling like you've given enough to others to "deserve" it for yourself.

Your mindsets matter. The more you keep these beliefs in mind, the more you will be able to help yourself ask for and accept help. As former US President Barack Obama remarked, "Don't be afraid to ask for help when you need it. I do that every day. Asking for help isn't a sign of weakness, it's a sign of strength. It shows you have the courage to admit when you don't know something, and to learn something new."

CHAPTER 5: REVIEW AND REFLECT

 REVIEW:

- Trying to get everything done without help from others has serious ramifications to our physical, mental, emotional, reputational, and interpersonal wellbeing.

- When you believe that you should be able to do everything without asking for help, your confirmation bias will actively look for evidence to support this perspective.

- Adopting a *growth mindset*, an *appreciative mindset*, a *resourceful mindset*, and a *hopeful mindset* can help you shift to healthier beliefs and behaviors about asking for and accepting help.

 REFLECT:

- Who do you know at work or among your friends and family who seems to want to get everything done without asking for help? How might you share this observation with them in a morally neutral, non-judgmental way?

- In what parts of your work or life do you tend to try to go it alone, even when you have an inkling that asking for and accepting help from someone else could relieve some of your stress? What mindset shifts might you consider making?

CHAPTER 6:

OTHER PEOPLE ARE WANTING AND WAITING TO HELP YOU

You've probably had a thought (or many thoughts) that stopped you from asking for help. Maybe it was, *I don't want to bother people.* Or, *Everybody is busy, too.* Or, *I should be able to handle this myself.* Or, *I don't want to make someone feel guilty if they have to say no.*

You can see how those beliefs might stop you in your tracks, right? You might even think to yourself, *Why would someone want to help me, especially if it doesn't benefit them?*

Here's why:

EVOLUTION HAS MADE HUMANS HELPFUL CREATURES.

We have evolved as a species to be prosocial creatures, where offering and receiving help have actually helped us to survive.

Evolutionarily speaking, humans had to help others as a mechanism for survival. If person A helps person B forage for berries, it is likely that when person A is in need of food, person B will provide them with some of their resources. This is what's called "reciprocal altruism," whereby people help one another with the expectation that if they need help in the future, someone will return the favor. The more our ancestors helped others, the more they were helped in return, which means there is a greater chance for them to survive and reproduce.

Reciprocal altruism shows up in many ways in modern times. If your neighbor mows your lawn for you, you might feel inclined to water their plants for them when they are away. If your boss gives you an extension on a deadline, you may turn your proposal in early the next time.

When Sophie started a thrift resale business during her sophomore year at Duke, she would purchase clothing at Goodwill and sell it online for a profit. One day, a woman whose daughter attended Virginia Tech reached out to Sophie to ask her about some Virginia Tech jerseys that Sophie had listed online. When the woman came to Sophie's house to select what she wanted for her daughter, she was torn between two items. Sophie decided to give her both jerseys for the price of one, partially because she wanted to get rid of her excess inventory (self-help), and partially because she knew that college apparel is expensive (helping others). What she didn't know was that this customer would demonstrate reciprocal altruism. The woman told Sophie that because of the generous deal Sophie offered her, she would drop off her own clothes for Sophie to sell—without asking for a cut of the profits.

Deb has experienced this as well. When she was first beginning her consulting business, she volunteered to offer no-cost instructional design and training delivery services to a workforce development program in New York City. One of her co-volunteers, Randy, appreciated the quality of Deb's work, and offered to introduce her to his boss at a Fortune 50 company. As a result of this introduction, Deb got her first big training engagement. Almost two decades later, in the middle of the pandemic, Randy, who was now also an independent consultant, reached out to Deb to share that he was having a tough time transitioning his business to an online environment. Could she help him brainstorm some ideas? Deb was both flattered that he reached out to her, and eager to return the help he had given her so many years ago that boosted her career trajectory. Her answer, of course, was yes.

As organizational psychologist and Wharton Professor Adam Grant writes in his book *Give and Take: A Revolutionary Approach to Success*, giving is contagious. It appears to create a safe space in group settings for people to adopt giving behaviors with less concern that others will take advantage of them.

Humans are naturally prosocial creatures. Those who have turned this tendency into a career include firefighters, police officers, soldiers, and others in both traditional and non-traditional helping professions. Many of these people risk their lives to help others, and while your boss or friend may not be willing to make the ultimate sacrifice, they are likely compelled to help other people in some way. And that includes you.

So, the next time you think to yourself, *I have nobody but myself to count on,* remind yourself that it is in our DNA to want to help others.

WANTING TO HELP YOU AND KNOWING HOW TO HELP YOU AREN'T THE SAME THING.

If most people want to help, and you are willing to be helped, what's in the gap?

One reason why a friend, family member, or colleague might not be helping you is because they may not know which helping approach to use. This could mean that they think there are too many options, too few options, or they are too focused on "getting it right" that they don't end up helping at all.

Think of this as similar to writer's block—let's call it "helper's block."

When a writer has writer's block, they are not able to write any new material, possibly because they don't know where to start (too many options), they have no ideas (too few options), or because they are paralyzed by the thought that what they write needs to be perfect (Sophie and Deb recognize this tension firsthand). As a result, nothing gets written, the pressure mounts, and feelings of guilt and anxiety ensue. "Helper's block" follows the same pattern.

And what does having too many options look like?

Let's say you just ended a long-term romantic relationship, and your friend wants to help you through this difficult time. They may be wrestling with these options:

"Should I bring cookies? Should I recommend a therapist? Does she want space or would she prefer company? Should I share my own experience—or make sure she knows this is not about me? I don't know how to help!"

The last statement, "I don't know how to help," is a classic verisimilitude. It's not true, but it *feels* true. Your friend does know how to help. They just named six ways they could help you, and for those who are counting, they are:

1. Bring cookies

2. Recommend a therapist

3. Offer space

4. Offer company

5. Share their experience

6. Focus on you, not them

This is what is known as "overchoice" or "choice overload," where having too many options can cause people to be indecisive, and eventually, not take action at all.

Another possibility of why someone isn't showing up to help you is that they feel they have too few options.

Your friend might be thinking, *There's nothing I can do to help someone who is grieving.* If they think that, they may feel like they have no options and will not help.

Your friend also might be thinking, *No matter how I help, something is bound to go wrong. What if I bring cookies but they are the wrong kind? Or what if I recommend a therapist and they turn out to be a mismatch? What if I say something that makes my friend upset?*

This kind of thought pattern can become obsessive, and it happens when a person wants to help so much that they worry too much about not helping in the exact right way. These ruminations can be paralyzing, and can lead someone to step back rather than step in.

While it's possible someone isn't helping you because they don't know which way to help, it's also possible that they don't know how to approach *you*.

Not every relationship is clear cut. You may be friendly with your manager, but are you actually *friends*? Your dad might be your confidante, but he's also your parent. Your new partner may be a wonderful person for dinner, drinks, and movies, but you've also only known each other for three weeks. These can be relationship dynamics to manage. And that's why the lack of clarity in how you and the other person define your relationship can make it hard for them to offer help in an appropriate way.

Or maybe, just maybe, someone has tried to help you in the past and it didn't go so well. It might be hard for that person to approach you again in the future, not knowing if you want their help, whether you will accept help from them, or take it the wrong way.

It's tricky to figure out how to help someone with whom we've had a confusing or challenging relationship. It's also hard to offer help to someone who is "help reserved" (it takes a lot of cognitive and emotional effort for them to ask for help) or "help resistant" (it takes a lot of cognitive and emotional effort for them to accept help).

When Deb herniated a disc in her lower back doing a beginner's yoga class on YouTube (don't ask), she was unable to walk without a cane for several days until she could get a cortisone injection. Those several days corresponded with her husband Michael being out of town on business. And while Deb could do most things around the house without his help, one thing she couldn't do was walk their 80 lb. rescue pit bull, Nash. Nash is notoriously hard to walk under the best of circumstances—she is somehow both as slow as molasses and yet fast as lightning when she sees a cat, rabbit, or squirrel. But these were not the best of circumstances, with Deb hobbling slowly and painfully.

So Deb reached out to her local dog walking company and made arrangements for them to come four times a day for the next three days. At $17 per walk, it wasn't cheap, but at least it would be handled.

When Deb's neighbors and local family members called her to see how she was feeling, and to ask what they could do to help, she reported that she wasn't feeling great, but that she had everything under control. "But what about Nash?" several of them asked. "You can't walk her, and Michael is going away."

When Deb reported that she had hired dog walkers to help with Nash, every single one of her local friends and family members said some version of "That's ridiculous!" and they also asked some version of "Why didn't you ask me?"

Deb didn't have a great answer for that other than, "I didn't want to bother you." But, as she would quickly learn, her tribe was way more bothered that she didn't feel comfortable asking them.

By the end of that week, Deb had learned that her reluctance to ask for help wasn't an asset. In fact, it was a hindrance to her personally, and to her relationships with those whom she had helped out in the past (and who were looking forward to the reciprocity). And also, by the end of that week, Nash had been walked entirely by a rotating team of unpaid volunteers—including Deb's friends Leslie, Gary, and Amy, her brother-in-law Jonathan, and her father-in-law Archie.

If you, like Deb, are or have been someone who is "help resistant" or "help reserved," someone who really, truly wants to help you might become resistant or reserved about offering over time. They may worry about possible negative reactions on your end, or they may think they will offend you, or make the situation worse. They may also not want to pressure you into getting help by offering you help. And nobody wants to be rejected. All of these are reasons why the people who are wanting and waiting to help you might not be offering.

WHEN YOU DON'T ASK FOR HELP, PEOPLE MAKE ASSUMPTIONS.

When you don't ask for help, it's likely that someone else will think one of three things: *They're fine; They don't trust me;* or *Our relationship is not there yet.*

Let's break down some of these assumptions.

They're fine.

When you don't ask for help, it is possible that someone will just think that you are fine without them. This could mean that they believe that you don't need help or that you are getting help elsewhere. This could be problematic if you actually need their help, right?

Let's say you are working from home and your kids are too young to occupy themselves. You probably need some help with childcare while you are working. If you don't ask others for help, they may think that you can handle it on your own or you already have childcare handled. If neither of these are true, your inaction ensures that you don't get the help you need. And you're likely left tired, frustrated, and unable to be at your best with your colleagues and your kids.

They don't trust me.

When you don't ask someone for help, they may think that you don't trust them. This is a common assumption that people make, especially anxious people (like Deb and Sophie), and it is a challenging feeling to sit with. No one wants to believe that someone else doesn't trust them.

This assumption can mean a lot of things as well. If you're not asking for help, someone might believe that you think they are incapable of helping. Going back to the childcare example, if Deb is your friend and she knows you are struggling with childcare and you don't ask her for help, Deb might think that you think she doesn't have the skill necessary to help. This would most likely make Deb feel hurt—especially since she has raised two amazing children!

Deb might also believe that because you didn't ask her for help, you think she's unwilling to help. She might also believe that you think it's too vulnerable to ask her for help. Deb might then think that she did something wrong, or that she's unapproachable or intimidating.

While Deb might also have other assumptions, she is also likely to make this one:

We're not there yet.

You probably wouldn't ask someone you've only known for a week to help you move into your new apartment. You also probably wouldn't ask someone you've just fought with in front of the entire office to drive you to the airport. This makes sense because your relationship is either not there or not there yet.

When there is a mismatch between the ask and your relationship with the person, it's valid for the other person to assume you're not asking them for help because "we're not there yet." But often, when you don't ask someone for help when you really do have a good relationship with them, this assumption that they may make can feel hurtful.

After Sophie published her first book *Don't Tell Me to Relax!: One Teen's Journey to Survive Anxiety (And How You Can Too)*, many family members were surprised by the stories she told about struggling with mental illness. Sophie had kept a lot of her pain and anxiety to herself, so much so that her twin brother, Jake, had no idea she even had an anxiety disorder.

The same thing was true with Sophie's uncle and grandpa. Sure, they both knew Sophie was dealing with a lot of stress and was in therapy, but they weren't aware of just how much Sophie had been struggling (panic attacks, side effects of medication, thinking about dropping out of high school, etc.). After reading the book, both of them, while feeling incredibly proud of Sophie, also felt hurt.

Why? Because they assumed that Sophie didn't reach out to them for help because she thought she didn't have a good enough relationship with them. Sophie knew it had nothing to do with her relationship with them, but the damage had been done and it was time to clean up the mess she made.

You don't ever want to make someone you're close with feel like the relationship is one-sided. When you don't ask the people whom you trust for help, they may believe that your relationship with them isn't as strong as they thought it was.

While none of us can control how someone else feels, you do have the ability to influence the assumptions people make about you. You don't want others to assume you see them as unavailable or untrustworthy, so either ask them for help (even when it feels hard or scary), or make sure you let them know *why* you aren't asking them for help. Otherwise, you can assume that they'll be making up a story about how you really feel about them—and it's not likely to be a happy story.

IDENTIFY THE KIND OF HELP YOU NEED.

Now that you understand why people want to help you and the assumptions people make when you don't ask for the help you need, it's time to identify the kind of help you need and the kind of help you don't need.

As poet Shel Silverstein wrote,

"Some kind of help is the kind of help

That helping's all about,

And some kind of help is the kind of help

We all can live without."

You have a role in thinking about and asking for the former kind of help, so that you're not stuck trying to dodge the latter kind.

And while you have myriad options for help, it can be helpful to simplify it into two categories, popularized by leadership authors Paul Hersey and Ken Blanchard:

1. Direction

   and

2. Support

Direction is "go there," "do this," or "try that." At its best, direction is assertive, practical, and clear. It's for when you are developing a skill or competency and need instructions, advice, clear goals, deadlines, examples of what "good" looks like, and frequent feedback on your progress so you can (hopefully) learn to do it all by yourself at some point.

When you were learning to drive, you needed your instructor to tell you when to lean on the gas, when to hit the brake, how to stay on your side of the road, what maneuvers were legal and safe, etc. It would not have been helpful for your instructor to say, "I'm sure you've seen plenty of driving before. Show me what you know!" (And we certainly would not have wanted to be on the road with you if that were their approach.)

At work, it could be your colleague telling you exactly how to make a request from your grumpy, world-weary administrative assistant that will get it handled with minimal pushback. At home, it could be asking someone else to decide what's for dinner tonight, and then please also make that dinner—by 6:30 pm.

Direction can also be "step aside—I've got this." When there's a skill or competency you're not planning to develop, you may need someone to just do it for you. And so, you step aside to create space for that to happen. This could be anyone from your accountant (if you're not totally up-to-date on local and federal tax laws), or Deb's mother (whose chicken soup with parsnips magically cures everything, and you want a quart just made for you).

"Step aside—I've got this" help is also for when there's something you know how to do, but you just can't do it right now.

Deb was in the middle of designing and delivering a year-long leadership development program with her colleagues when her mother-in-law Joan passed away after a brief but painful battle with lung cancer. Before taking time off to be with her family to sit shiva (the seven days of customary Jewish mourning), Deb called her colleague Jennifer to assure her that she would get the next draft of the program delivered ASAP. Jennifer's response to Deb was, "Stop working. We've got this. Go be with your family."

While it was hard for Deb to accept the help because she really wanted to deliver for her teammates, she also knew that Jennifer's help was being offered genuinely and with no strings attached. She also knew that the next iteration of the program might not be exactly what she had envisioned, but that it would be excellent, nonetheless. And finally, Deb also knew that if she didn't accept Jennifer's help, she wouldn't be able to help the rest of her family through this sad time.

And what kind of help was Deb offering her family through loss and grief? Support—not direction. It wasn't "Here's how long to grieve for" (especially since grief is an adaptive challenge), or "This is when we should start donating her jackets to the thrift store." It was the kind of help that Joan's family and friends were able to deliver masterfully. It included really listening, holding space, being empathetic, focusing on happy times even in the midst of sadness, and so much more.

Needing support isn't just for emotionally fraught situations like illness and death. You might have to have a challenging conversation with a demanding client—and while you don't need your boss to tell you *how* to have that talk, you could use a pep talk for yourself. Or you might have three job offers come in within a week (and congratulations!). You don't need your brother to advise you on which one to accept, but you could use a gentle reminder that you have a track record of making excellent decisions.

While direction is pointing the way, removing obstacles that are in your way, or you getting out of the way entirely so someone else can get it handled, support is helping you find your own way—in good times and in bad.

So, take a moment and think about a challenge you're facing right now, at work, at home, or elsewhere. What would be more helpful right now? Direction (someone telling you what to do, how to do it, or doing it for you)? Or support (someone empathizing, listening, or cheering you on)? Or do you maybe need a sampler platter—a little bit of both?

IDENTIFY WHO SHOULD HELP YOU.

You have probably figured out by now what kind of help you need. The next step is to determine who you should ask for help.

The process for determining who you should ask for help will sound familiar from Chapter 3:

1. **Who is able?** If you need *direction*, think about who knows how to do this task well—and has a proven track record. When Deb needs help getting herself organized (which is embarrassingly often), she usually taps her husband Michael for help. Why? Because he is organized himself (his sock drawer is a work of art), and he has a background as an engineer and a project manager. He has the credentials, the personal credibility, and the experience to help her with this.

   If you need *support,* consider who has supported you in the past in a way that felt like they were making it about you, not them. Or who has supported you in the way you needed in that particular situation. Deb's friend Wendy is a top-notch supporter in this way. When Deb has a personal or professional setback, she knows that when she calls Wendy, she'll say, "Oh, honey… that's terrible!" Wendy won't try to get Deb to see the bright side, or focus on silver linings, or offer unsolicited advice. She will just be present and empathetic. And this is not a skill set that everyone has right now (but they can develop it by reading this book!).

   It's your turn: Think about a situation, challenge, dilemma, or opportunity where you could use some help. If it's direction you need, who has a track record in doing this task well? Who has the training (formal or informal)? Who just "gets it done" and can help you do that too? If you need support, who has shown that they can meet you where you are emotionally? Who will flex their approach based on what you need? Who won't try to cheer you up prematurely? Who won't continue to ruminate with you once you're ready to move on?

2. Who is willing? Once you've identified who *can* help, think about who *will* help you—at the time you need it. You may want your manager to walk you through how to write a performance plan for your direct report, but if she's knee-deep in her own performance assessments, she may not have capacity to help right now. (Yes, even if it's her job to help you.) You may want your partner to help you choose the most flattering swimsuit for your summer trip to Greece, but if they're just sitting down to watch the season finale of *The Crown*, you're not going to get the support you need when you need it.

Willingness is also about more than timing and capacity. It's also about confidence. Asking someone for help who doesn't believe that they know enough or have enough experience to be helpful can feel frustrating—for both of you. So, you may need to help them help you, by reminding them that you see their knowledge and experience as valuable to you. For example, you might want some writing advice from your colleague, and saying "I know you say you've only written one book, but I haven't written any books yet, so you're already ahead of me" could inspire their willingness to help.

It's also about motivation. Early on in Deb's career as a coach and consultant, she reached out to a close colleague for his help on getting her business launched. She was surprised to discover that this colleague was not motivated to help her; in fact, he saw Deb as competition to his own consulting practice, and didn't want to offer any direction or support that he thought could negatively impact his business.

This stung Deb deeply. It felt like a breach of trust. It also became a tremendous motivator for Deb to run her business with as much professional generosity as she possibly could. As a result of this painful experience, she is usually happy to offer fellow consultants tips and tools for growing their own businesses.

Now it's up to you: Think about the help you need. Who do you know who may have the time, the capacity, the motivation, and the confidence to help you? And if you find yourself making up a story in your head that *she's too busy* or *he won't think he can help me*, do yourself (and them) a favor and ask anyway. You can and will survive being told "no," but if you don't ask, you definitely will not get what you need.

3. **Who can you count on?** Now that you have a better sense of who can help and is willing to help, you're almost done. But there's one more factor to consider: who can you really count on to show up for you in the way you need it?

Consider this: your best friend may be *able* to drive you to the airport on Tuesday morning, and is *willing* to drive you to the airport on Tuesday morning... and he is also late every single time you make a plan. Do you really want his "help" on Tuesday morning, or would you rather call a taxi?

And this: your manager is *able* to give you feedback on your client pitch and is *willing* to give you feedback on your client pitch... and she has a track record of making vague statements like "Nice job!" Do you really want to keep asking her for feedback on your pitch, or could you ask a colleague whom you know is clearer and more direct?

When it comes to asking for help, you want to ask someone whom you trust to be sincere (tells the truth and considers the impact), reliable (honors their commitments), competent (knows how to do what they're supposed to do), and caring (thinks about your needs, values, and interests).

And you don't need someone to be all of these things in all areas for every piece of help you need. You need your car mechanic to be reliable and competent, and you'd probably sacrifice a bit of caring to get your car fixed quickly. Deb's husband Michael considers her "unskilled" when it comes to loading the dishwasher, but he relies on her sincerity when he asks for feedback on his writing.

Think about it: for the help you need right now, who can you count on? And better yet, who *else* can you count on in case you need help from more than one person, or the original person wasn't as available as you'd hoped?

MAKING THE REQUEST FOR HELP.

Once you've decided who, it's time to ask. And, like so many other things, getting in the right mindset about asking is the first step. Then, take a few minutes to reflect on your past successes. You can ask yourself, "When I've asked this person for help before, what made the request successful?"

Think about what may have contributed to it. Was it good timing? Maybe you approached your boss for help on a Friday afternoon when she was already relaxed for the weekend ahead. Was it word choice? Perhaps you asked your son for "a huge favor, and I won't forget that you helped me out" —and you knew that he was putting that help deposit in the bank for later. Perhaps it was body language. You had a serious expression on your face when you asked your colleague for coverage at work—and that facial expression communicated how urgently you needed his help. In Michael's family (Deb's in-laws), people are less likely to want to help when the request is vague ("Hey, what are you doing on Saturday?") vs. specific ("Hey, do you think you could help me move a table from upstairs to downstairs on Saturday afternoon?").

(It's become a family joke that "Hey, what are you doing on Saturday?" means you're about to ask for help with something that *nobody* wants to help with.)

And perhaps it was the relationship itself: you're just both committed to helping each other grow and develop.

Of course, you don't want to get into "analysis-paralysis" —where you're so focused on reverse-engineering your requests for help that you don't actually get to the ask!

Here are ten ways to start the conversation (and of course, make the topics your own):

1. "I could really use your help on getting the kids to bed earlier. Can we discuss how we can make this happen?"

2. "Do you remember when we talked about me taking over payroll? Well, I'm working on it and I need some specific help. Is now a good time, or is there a better time?"

3. "I could use a pep talk right now before I call my parents about our holiday plans. Are you free?"

4. "Asking for help is hard for me, but I feel comfortable asking you…"

5. "I thought that I could install this light fixture myself. I can't. Can you recommend someone to help me?"

6. "I am feeling frustrated, and I just need to vent. I don't need any advice or problem solving—just a few minutes to get things off my chest. Will you do this with me?"

7. "Our organization needs someone to volunteer to raise money for the annual event. Can you help with this?

Or is there some other way in which you'd prefer to help?"

8. "I need to get better at asking for help, and I'm starting now. Can I tell you what I need?"

9. "I know that ruminating about my dad's cognitive decline isn't going to help him. I could use a distraction. Will you do that for me?"

10. "I have to decide which apartment to rent by the end of day tomorrow. Will you help me make a pros-and-cons list?"

ASKING FOR HELP IN A TRICKY RELATIONSHIP.

A quick reality check here: Sometimes we need to ask for help from people where the relationship isn't secure or mature. It's not ideal, but it's real. If your answer to the earlier question about what made the ask work is "Nothing—it was a miserable conversation and we both felt horrible during and afterward," you have a few choices:

First, you can acknowledge that in this conversation. You can say, "I remember that the last time I asked you for help, we both left the discussion feeling angry and frustrated. I'd like to hear from you how I contributed to your feeling that way. Would you share with me what I could have done differently?" And then be open to getting feedback without defensiveness. You just might learn something about your own approach that could use an upgrade.

Second, you can approach someone else who has a better track record of getting help from this person. The goal of this conversation is not to vent or gossip. This is not a "I have to ask Kamal for help with the budget, and I know he's going to blow up at me" conversation. It should be focused on getting specific strategies for asking for help from Kamal from someone who has done it before—and more successfully than you. Try, "I know that you and Kamal have a good working relationship. I would like to get better at asking him for help. What approach do you use?" (And then thank your colleague for their help rather than telling them why "that won't work.")

Third, you can figure out how to work around them. It tends to take extra time and effort, but unless they're the only person in the organization, or your family, or your community who can help with what you need, find a different path.

And if you're new to asking this person for help, you can say that to them, too. "I've never come to you for help before—and I realize I don't know the best way to make a request. Should I just go for it, or do you have some preferences?"

When it comes to asking, there's no one right way, and there's no one wrong way. There are *lots* of wrong ways!

Here are six approaches to avoid:

Quid Pro Quo: "I need help. And just to remind you, you owe me."

Last Hope: "I asked everyone else I know, and nobody could help me. So, I am coming to you…"

Guilt: "After all I've done for you, the least you can do is help me."

Manipulative: "Do you think you could stop focusing on yourself for once and help me?"

Sarcastic: "Yeah, like you'd really ever help me!"

Insult: "I know you're not great at this either, but maybe you can help me anyway…"

And you probably have several from your own experience! All of these examples are great ways to *not* get the help you want, and to damage the relationship down the road.

Let's assume good news: you've asked, and they've agreed. Thank them, be specific with your expectations, discuss any possible roadblocks, and then let them help you.

And let's also address the bad news. What if the ask goes wrong?

Here are six scenarios of an ask gone wrong, and some ideas about what to do:

1. **You ask for help and they say no.** In this case, you can thank them for hearing your request and ask for an explanation of their response. Or you can thank them and express your disappointment and/or your understanding. Or you can just thank them and move on.

2. **You ask for help and they get angry at you for asking.** Notice and name what you hear and see, using morally neutral language. It could sound like, "It seems to me like you're upset with me for asking. Did I get that right? I'd like to understand what about my asking for help bothered you." And then listen for any information or feedback that can help you reframe your ask now, or give you a higher chance of success down the road.

3. **You ask for help and they express judgment for you needing help**. Similar to the example above, notice and name what you hear and see, and share the impact that their reaction is having on you. Try, "It feels to me like when I asked you for help, your response was telling me why I shouldn't need help. The impact on me is that I feel like I won't be able to ask you for help in the future out of fear that you'll judge me negatively for asking. Was that what you intended?"

4. **You ask for help, they say yes, and you feel (pretty) certain that they can't or don't want to help.** This is a good opportunity to bring yourself in as an example. You might say, "I appreciate you offering to help me. And I also get the sense that you're not sure if you really can right now. I know that I sometimes say yes to helping someone without really thinking it through. Would you like to think about it and we can check back in tomorrow?" And then, follow up and accept their final answer.

5. **You ask for help, they say yes, and then they don't help you.** It's easy to make up a story here: they didn't really want to help in the first place; they resent you; you're not a priority to them. But all you know is the fact: they didn't help. The rest is made up in your head. Stop making up a story and just ask them: "When we spoke last week, you agreed to edit my proposal by the end of this week. It's now Friday, and the proposal hasn't been edited. I've made up a story in my head that you have more important things to work on, but I'd rather get the real story. Will you share with me what's going on?"

6. **You ask for help, they say yes, and then the help is unhelpful.** One reason why this can happen is because you weren't clear in requesting what help you really needed (or you didn't confirm clarity on their end). In this case, you might say, "Thank you for agreeing to help me set some deadlines. I realize now that what I was really requesting was you helping me think through what deadlines I should set for myself, rather than you telling me what my deadlines should be. I should have been clearer with you about that. Are you open to helping me think it through that way?"

Another reason may be because something shifted along the way—their ability, willingness, or the relationship. In which case, you might just need to get curious: "When I asked you to teach me your process for developing a workshop, you said you'd sit down with me for two hours and walk me through it. Instead, you sent me several decks of workshop materials for me to analyze on my own. Will you help me understand what changed?"

Asking for help can be as simple as saying "I could use a hand. Are you available?" And, at times, it may be more complicated, especially if you're waiting to feel like you deserve to be helped, or that you have to ask the perfect person, or that your request needs to be flawless. Nevertheless, recognizing that humans are wired to want to help each other (and that includes you) is a helpful first step in getting better at asking for the help you want and need.

CHAPTER 6: REVIEW AND REFLECT

REVIEW:

- We are biologically and evolutionarily wired to be prosocial—engaging in behavior that is positive, helpful, and intended to promote social bonding.

- When you don't ask for help from the people around you who are wanting and waiting to help you, they may make some erroneous (and painful) assumptions about how you see their competency, or how you view your relationship.

- When you do ask for help, be clear about what kind of help you're looking for—and what doesn't feel particularly helpful to you.

REFLECT:

- How can you make it easier for someone in your work or life to ask you for help? What might you say or not say to them that could help them feel more comfortable and confident in their ask of you?

- Whose help do you want to start asking for, because they likely can and will help you? And whose help comes with strings attached or other problematic elements? How can you change that dynamic or stop asking them for their assistance?

PART 2:

THE HELP STRATEGIES

Now that you know how to offer help, how to ask for help, and how to accept help, it's time to get clear on the specific help strategies. Here are 31 ways to offer the help your friends, colleagues, and family members need—as well as ask for what you need, too.

Get curious

1. Listen to learn
2. Find the focus
3. Interrupt their story—strategically
4. Ask powerful questions

Offer support

5. Empathize
6. Invite them to admit something vulnerable
7. Help them tolerate discomfort and ambiguity
8. Summon their strengths
9. Raise the bar for them
10. Help them focus on what is working

Give direction

11. Tell them what to do
12. Take something off their plate
13. Do it with them, side by side
14. Teach them how to do something
15. Recommend an approach to try
16. Recommend what to avoid

17. Offer resources

18. Share your own experience

Plan and execute

19. Set S.M.A.R.T. and S.M.A.R.T.E.S.T. goals

20. Action planning

21. Anticipating and overcoming obstacles

22. Point out "solution aversion"

23. Challenge catastrophic thinking

24. Reflect on blind spots

25. Encourage commitment and accountability

Evaluate and celebrate

26. Offer helpful feedback

27. Evaluate both process and performance

28. Help them see their progress

29. Invite self-evaluation

30. Promote the pause

31. Celebrate

CHAPTER 7:

GET CURIOUS

Picture this: It's 3:37 am and your baby is crying. Very, very loudly. (If you're Deb in this scenario, it was two crying babies at once!) You check your baby's diaper to see if he's wet or dirty. Nope. You feed him, but he won't eat. You look to see if there's a tag in his onesie that's bothering him, or if there's something stuck in his tiny nostrils making it hard for him to breathe, or if he scratched himself in the night. No, no, and no. So you just hold him in your arms and rock him, and he quickly falls back to sleep.

What did he need? He just needed your physical presence.

And despite the fact that this scenario involved an infant, many of us at all ages are in a similar situation to both the parent and the baby.

How so?

We don't always know what the real problem is for the other person, and so we don't know how to help. And we don't always know what we need for ourselves, so we don't know what help to ask for.

And rather than using our time, energy, and resources to try a dozen ways of helping before we hit on something that works, we can just get curious.

What does it mean to be curious?

It means that we don't know what the real challenge, dilemma, or opportunity is, and we want to know so that we can be helpful *in the way that works best for the other person*. It means that we put ourselves in a learner mindset (there's that word again), where we decide to put aside our existing knowledge, judgments, and biases so that we can start fresh with this person and this situation.

HELP STRATEGY 1
LISTEN TO LEARN

Deb and Sophie both love to talk. As professional speakers, they both talk for a living. However, when they are trying to help a client, a colleague, a friend, family member or each other, they shift their focus from talking to listening.

Listening can be a lot harder than talking—and it's one of the best ways of helping others.

Studies show that when you feel listened to, you:

- Get a clearer picture of who you are
- Increase your self-awareness and self-knowledge
- Clarify your thinking
- Challenge your own thinking, beliefs, and perspectives
- Are more likely to relax and share your inner thoughts and feelings without worrying about being judged by others.

Do you see how listening can be such a valuable helping strategy? And in order to do it well, you first need to recognize what's likely to get in your way.

RECOGNIZE WHAT GETS IN THE WAY OF YOUR LISTENING.

One reason why listening is so tricky is that we are all distracted by both *outside noise* and *inside noise*. *Outside noises* are the external distractions that we are surrounded by every day at work and at home that drive inattention: external conversations, email chimes, cell phones ringing, interruptions. *Internal noises* are the voices in our heads that distract us from truly paying attention to the person we're supposed to be listening to so that we can help them: worries we have; advice we want to give; explanations we want to offer; reasons why they're wrong, etc.

Internal noises also include voices of bias. They're often unconscious—but they're there, getting in the way of our being able to really listen deeply, equitably, and without judgment. We might listen more to someone who is a lot like us (based on the similarity bias), or to someone we've seen or spoken to more recently (an expression of the distance bias), or even to someone who is alerting us to a potential risk or danger (because of our safety bias). And one of the most common biases is known as the closeness-communication bias. This is where you actually listen the least to the people you know the best. After all, if you know them so well, you can already predict what they're going to say, right?

Alternatively, we may unconsciously pay less attention to those unlike ourselves—whether it's because they don't share the same degree as us, the same first language, professional status, or country of origin.

And to be clear, you're probably not aware that this is happening. And that's what makes these biases even more important to be mindful of.

Both external and internal noises keep us from committing to really hearing what's being said—and often, what's being left unsaid—by the people we are supposed to be helping.

As Joseph Grenny, *The New York Times* best-selling author of *Crucial Conversations*, wrote: "If you don't talk it out, you act it out."

Another reason that listening is challenging is that very few of us have ever been formally taught listening skills. Think about it: how many math classes, science classes, and language classes did you take in school? Probably dozens. Now how many listening classes did you take? If you're like most people, the answer is somewhere between one and none.

But it's not too late to learn!

Before you explore two ways to listen well, you should keep an eye (and ear) out for these habits that will prevent you from really listening—and really helping:

- You already believe you know better than other person does
- You already have advice to give
- You can predict how their story turns out
- You're paying attention only to the parts of what they're saying that interest you, confirm what you already know, or believe
- You're already planning your reply, rebuttal, defense, or counterattack.

If any of these sound familiar, you're not alone. And you have some work to do! Keep reading.

LISTEN WITH YOUR EARS AND YOUR EYES.

As you know, listening involves your ears. You need to listen for both what the other person is saying as well as what they're not saying. You also need to listen with your eyes, by watching for body language cues and clues.

To do this well, you really need to pay attention.

Paying attention requires two things: *tuning in* and *tuning out*.

By *tuning in* to the other person, you're demonstrating that they're the complete, undivided focus of your attention. You can do this by making eye contact, leaning forward toward them (yes, even over video), nodding when they speak, and lightly mirroring their facial expressions. And don't rush them.

You might say something like this: "I'm not going anywhere, so please take your time. I really want to understand what's going on so I can help."

You can also tune in to the content of what they're saying by paraphrasing them, and noticing shifts in body language. For example, your colleague might say something like this: "While I'm so excited to have this new, expanded role in the company, I also feel like I should be available to my team around the clock!"

To which you might respond: "When you said you were 'excited' about your new role, you frowned. Did you notice that, too?"

Tuning in also means paying attention to signs that the other person is done talking about a hard or vulnerable topic. If their sentences start getting shorter, or they're no longer making eye contact, or sending other signals that they're done for now, tune into that.

You might say something like this: "I'm getting the sense that you may want to wrap this up now. Is that right? And if so, how can I be most helpful?"

And then, follow their lead—and keep the door open for future conversations. They may want help, but not right now. (And for the record, letting them know that you're available to talk again is a way of helping.)

As for tuning out... turn off to tune out. Turn off your cell phone. Turn off your email chime. Turn off your TV or music. Turn off the soup on the stove if you're working from home.

And turn off the voices in your head. Turn off your filters: right/wrong; true/not true; important/not important; my problem/not my problem.

By recognizing what gets in the way of your listening, listening with your eyes and your ears, and listening for what people value, you'll be able to help people figure out the kind of help they want and need. And better yet, sometimes all the help that someone needs is to be listened to so that they can better understand themselves, their thinking, and what they want next.

HELP STRATEGY ❷
FIND THE FOCUS

One of the core principles of Appreciative Inquiry (which was discussed in Chapter 5) is known as the Poetic Principle: "What We Focus on Grows."

You've probably noticed this in multiple ways in your work and life, that when you put time, energy, and attention toward something, it tends to grow.

Like what?

Like improving your health, repairing your relationship with a sibling, increasing your savings, etc. And while focused attention isn't a guarantee that things will improve, few things will improve without it. But it can be hard to know what to focus on—especially when we're feeling stressed, overwhelmed, and confused.

When you help someone get clear on what *they* want to focus on (note: not *you*), you're really helping them to:

- Understand what's contributing to their stress (or excitement)

- Discover the real issue

- Identify options they didn't know they had

- Articulate what they want and need

- Clarify their priorities

- Choose what to put their time, energy, and attention toward, and decide what *not* to do.

And it doesn't have to be complicated.

SOMETIMES ALL YOU HAVE TO DO IS ASK, "WHAT DO YOU WANT TO FOCUS ON?"

Ed had been a brand manager in healthcare advertising for 12 years when he was laid off from his job. After six months of sending out resumes and cover letters, updating his LinkedIn profile, having calls and coffee with his network, and going on dozens of interviews, Ed was tired, frustrated, and disappointed.

"I'm feeling really defeated," he said to Deb in a coaching session. "I feel like I've tapped out my network, and I've lost my confidence. I don't know what to do next."

After Deb empathized with Ed, she asked him, "So, what would be most helpful to you right now to focus on? Growing your network, regaining your confidence, or something else?"

Ed took no more than ten seconds to think about it before responding, "Regaining my confidence. If I can do that, I think I can handle the rest myself."

So that's what Deb helped him with. She didn't offer to review his resume. She didn't suggest better ways to leverage LinkedIn. She gave him the help he asked for. And as you can see, in order for her to know what kind of help would be helpful to Ed, she needed to help him Find the Focus. In this case, it was regaining his confidence.

But what do you do if helping someone find their focus isn't as cut and dried?

FOR COMPLEX CHALLENGES, YOU NEED TO "CARVE THE TURKEY."

Picture this: it's a holiday meal, and you have friends and family sitting around the dining room table waiting to eat. You take the 15 lb. turkey you've been cooking for hours out of the oven, put it on a platter, and start to carry it to the dining room. This turkey is hot, heavy, and huge. It's hard to balance, it's pretty slippery, and by the time you get it to the table, you're exhausted.

"Alright, everyone," you announce, wiped out. "Eat!"

Your company looks at the turkey, and then they look at you, and then they look back at the turkey again. What's the problem? You didn't carve the turkey. And nobody can be expected to eat a 15 lb. turkey whole. Right?

Right.

This turkey is a metaphor for a problem, dilemma, or challenge that feels hot, heavy, and huge. Something that is so big that you can't digest it whole. You need to carve it into parts in order to even see the individual elements of this tricky situation, and then you need to decide which part you're going to put on your plate first, and then what the very first bite is.

"Carving the turkey" is a strategy to help you, your coworkers, friends, or family who are struggling with something overwhelming or complex to manage it more successfully, one bite at a time.

Here's what it could sound like:

Your colleague comes to you and says, "I'm feeling totally overwhelmed. We have this huge deadline coming up next week, and I'm still trying to virtually onboard our new hire. Our administrative assistant is on leave, so I'm doing a lot of scheduling and paperwork that's normally handled for me. To make it worse, my kid is getting up in the middle of the night with bad dreams, so I'm operating on about four hours of sleep. Oh, and I threw out my back this weekend doing yard work, so I can't even sit comfortably. I just don't know what to do!"

Chances are, if you heard your colleague share this situation, you would feel overwhelmed too! And you also might think to yourself, *How on earth am I supposed to help?*

Help them find the focus by looking at all of that as a turkey, and then help your colleague carve it into parts.

Here's what it could sound like:

"Wow! That is a lot. And I can completely understand how you'd be feeling overwhelmed. Let's see if we can separate that into its individual parts, so you can see more clearly what to do next."

And then, together with your colleague, see if you can name all the parts. From the example above you might name:

- You're feeling overwhelmed
- You have a huge deadline coming up next week
- You're virtually onboarding our new hire
- Our administrative assistant is on leave, so you're doing extra work
- Your kid is having bad dreams
- You're not getting enough sleep
- Your back hurts
- You can't sit comfortably.

(And if you're feeling bold, you can even ask, "What did we miss?")

Then, you might say to your colleague, "Since you can't deal with everything at once, what one part do you want to put on your plate first? It might be the thing that's easiest to deal with, or the one part which, if handled first, will make the other parts easier to deal with, or even the part you've been putting off too long."

And let them choose. Let's say, in this situation, your colleague picked, "I need to deal with my back because being in pain makes everything else harder."

To which you might reply, "Excellent. So, what's the first bite—the very next step you will take?"

(Probably "Call the doctor.")

Notice that you didn't tell them what they should focus on, or what to do, or what not to do. You helped them by letting them see their own challenge through a new, clearer lens—and then make their own decisions.

What about you? What turkeys are you trying to deal with right now? And who can help you carve it into parts so that you have a place to start?

Knowing how to help someone "carve their turkey" can help them make the unmanageable more manageable.

But sometimes, the person who needs help may feel like they're being attacked by a rafter of turkeys (nope, the term is not "flock." Who knew?). When this happens, they may go on, and on, and on… which makes finding the focus hard to do.

In this case, you can help them by interrupting them—carefully, politely, and strategically.

HELP STRATEGY ❸
INTERRUPT THEIR STORY STRATEGICALLY

While some cultures consider interrupting one another a polite and expected way of communicating, many of us think of interrupting as rude, aggressive, annoying, and even self-centered. And, regardless of culture, when it's used to shut someone up, shut someone down, or turn the focus back to ourselves, it certainly can be all of those things.

However, when it's used in service of helping someone get clear about what's going on, and what kind of help they need, it can be a strategic conversation tool.

Your positive intent matters, as does what you say and how you say it.

Imagine this *real* real-life scenario:

Sophie says to Deb:

"I feel like you're getting a lot more writing done than I am. I want to write but I don't have motivation. It's hard because you get to write around a schedule, but my schedule is less predictable. I also have other work to do, and when I am writing I feel like I'm not doing my other work. I know it will all get done, but if I want to have a day off tomorrow, I need to get all of my writing done today. Also, I need to write twice as much as I already have done—or more—for me to meet my writing goals for the week. And it's not just the writing. I've just been feeling tired, and like maybe I'm not the right person to write this book. And another thing is…"

As you can imagine, Deb really wants to help (especially since Sophie's willingness and ability to write directly impacts her, too). But the focus is not clear about what kind of help Sophie needs.

So, one way Deb can help Sophie is by asking "What kind of help do you need?" Another way is by naming turkey parts. And yet another way is by interrupting Sophie's story to help her clarify what's going on.

In order for this to be helpful rather than harmful, the intrusion needs to be polite, caring, and goal-oriented.

Compare these interruptions. You'll notice that Conversation 2 is more helpful (and respectful) than Conversation 1.

CONVERSATION 1

Sophie: "I feel like you're getting a lot more writing done than I am. I want to write but I don't have motivation. It's hard because you get to write around a schedule, but my schedule is less predictable. I also have other work to do, and when I am writing I feel like I'm not doing my other work. I know it will all get done, but if I want to have a day off tomorrow, I need to get all of my writing done today. Also…"

Deb: "Hold up, hold up. I can't follow you if you're speaking that fast!"

or:

"Wait a second. You committed to this! Are you trying to back out?"

or:

"I'm sure you'll figure it out. You always do."

CONVERSATION 2

Sophie: "I feel like you're getting a lot more writing done than I am. I want to write but I don't have motivation. It's hard because you get to write around a schedule, but my schedule is less predictable. I also have other work to do, and when I am writing I feel like I'm not doing my other work. I know it will all get done, but if I want to have a day off tomorrow, I need to get all of my writing done today. Also…"

Deb: "May I pop in for a moment? It sounds like you have more to say, and I want to make sure I am getting the main points…"

or:

"Before you continue, I want to make sure I understand what you've said so far…"

or:

"Hang on a second. There's a lot here and I don't want to miss anything."

Do you see the difference? Sophie certainly did.

Here are three other phrases you can use to help someone focus their thinking and speaking, after you've politely "popped in":

1. "What's the real issue for you here?"
2. "If you had to pick one thing for me to help you with, what would it be?"
3. "What's the most important piece for us to talk about right now?"

And there will be times when the best kind of help is to let someone vent. Even if it takes a while. Even if the focus isn't crystal clear. And even if you're not sure how to help next. (So keep reading.)

HELP STRATEGY ❹
ASK POWERFUL QUESTIONS

"If you don't understand, ask questions. If you're uncomfortable about asking questions, say you are uncomfortable about asking questions and then ask anyway.

It's easy to tell when a question is coming from a good place. Then listen some more.

Sometimes people just want to feel heard.

Here's to possibilities of friendship and connection and understanding."

Americanah by Chimamanda Ngozi Adichie

It's good to have answers. It helps us offer ideas and resources, it reinforces our credibility, and, let's face it, it makes us feel smart.

And yet, it's just as good—and sometimes even better—to have questions.

Whether you're helping a colleague handle a difficult client, or your partner navigate a tricky career decision, you might know what *you* would do in their situation. But you're not them. Your answers may not be relevant, relatable, or realistic for them.

Asking powerful questions is the key to helping other people tap into their own resourcefulness. It's a reminder that, with time, reflection, self-awareness, and support, they can come up with ideas, plans, choices, and decisions on their own.

What's even more powerful is that when people develop their own course of action, they are more likely to be committed to it and ensure accountability, rather than just complying with someone else's.

So, what makes a question powerful rather than just passable?

A powerful question:

- Stems from genuine curiosity, which means you don't already know the answer
- Stimulates reflective thinking
- Is thought-provoking
- Surfaces underlying assumptions and limiting beliefs
- Generates new possibilities
- Is about the other person and their perspective and experience, not about you.

Check out the difference between passable questions and powerful questions below.

Your team member says: "Whenever I ask Jaime for a project status update, he says, "I'll have it to you shortly"… but shortly can mean a day or a week. I never know when—or if—he's going to deliver. And I'm on a deadline!"

Passable questions include:

"Could you be clearer about your expectations?" This is giving advice in the form of a question.

"Why does this keep happening with you two?" This is blaming.

"Does Jaime think it's a problem?" This is about someone who isn't a part of this conversation.

Compare that with powerful questions:

"What's important to you about this?" This is about why it matters to the person you're helping.

"How would you like it to be instead?" This is about them envisioning what success could look like.

"What do you think is contributing to this?" This is about them brainstorming what might be getting in the way—without blame or shame.

You might also have noticed that the powerful questions were all open questions. What's an open question? It's a question that requires exploration and thinking, and can't be answered with a simple yes or no.

Think about the difference between these two questions. The first question (closed) can be answered with a yes or no. The second question (open) will inspire reflection and thinking.

Closed question:

Are you prepared to make changes?

Open question:

What changes are you prepared to make?

Of course, closed questions aren't inherently bad. They can be helpful when used strategically.

For example, closed questions can help you navigate conversational boundaries. When Deb's friend Dan mentioned that he was feeling uncharacteristically stressed at work, she asked him this question to gauge his interest in disclosing more: "Are you open to talking more about this?"

And since his answer was yes, Deb then moved on to open-ended questions. If he had said no, Deb would have left the door open to future conversations, but wrapped this conversation up.

When using closed questions as permission to press further, assume that a yes is a green light to proceed, and a no may be red light to stop pressing.

Here are some more additional hallmarks of a powerful question:

- They tend to start with "what" or "how" rather than "why." Why tends to force people to justify themselves, which can make them feel defensive.

Compare *why* vs. *what*:

Why are you failing math?

Vs.

What could you do differently to prepare for math tests?

- They are short, allowing for a wider range of possible responses.

Compare *long* vs. *short*:

What do you think you could try to get your dad to let you know whether he is hosting the holidays this year, or if he wants you to host instead?

Vs.

What else might work here?

- They don't judge the other person, helping them feel supported.

Compare *judging* vs. *neutral*:

Why aren't you and your sister smart enough to figure out how to stop fighting?

Vs.

What pattern do you notice?

- They don't lead the other person to a specific answer that you are looking for or hoping they give, and they don't give advice in the form of a question. (A good tip for this is that if your question starts with "could/couldn't you?", "should/shouldn't you?", "why don't you?", "can/can't you?", or "how about if you?", recognize that you're about to offer a piece of thinly veiled advice!)

Compare *advising* vs *exploring*

Couldn't you explain to your girlfriend that you resent it when she criticizes your clothing?

Vs.

What might have a better impact?

- Finally, they don't pry or pull away from the other person.

Like what?

Prying: "Don't you have a therapist you can talk to about your problems?"

Pulling away: "Would you just let me know when you get this handled?"

Asking powerful questions can be challenging, especially if you're used to leading other people to the answer you're looking for, or you're pressed for time, or if you're not sure that your team member, child, partner, friend, or parent really is resourceful enough to get something handled.

And it can be simple.

How would you find out, for example, what your boss feels is the most important outcome for Tuesday's client meeting?

You could ask: "What's the most important outcome for Tuesday's client meeting?"

How could you find out what your child's challenge is with their soccer coach?

You could ask: "What's your challenge with your soccer coach?"

(See? Easy! Now it's your turn!)

What could you ask to find out what resources your colleague has to get her project done on time?

(If your question was something like: "What resources do you have to get your project done on time?" you've got it!)

You can ask your spouse what they're worried about with their new manager, or what your sister's timing is for her home renovation, or what's getting in the way of your direct report making it to work on time.

Asking powerful questions is a critical skill to help others become self-directed and self-motivated, which will free you up to focus on what you need to get done, yourself.

Which, of course, is helping you help yourself, too!

CHAPTER 7: REVIEW AND REFLECT

REVIEW:

- Listening without distraction or judgment can help someone feel heard, supported, and understood.

- Asking someone powerful questions can invite new thinking, novel possibilities, and self-awareness.

- You may have to interrupt someone (thoughtfully and strategically) to help them focus on what matters most to them. You can also do this by helping them carve up seemingly overwhelming challenges into more manageable parts.

REFLECT:

- Think about someone in your work or life whom you've been trying to help by telling them what to do. How might you shift your approach to make space for curiosity?

- What is something you're wrestling with where you would benefit from someone really listening, asking powerful questions, and helping you find the focus of this issue? And who do you know who could do this with you?

CHAPTER 8:

OFFER SUPPORT

"Don't ever let someone tell you, you can't do something. Not even me. You got a dream, you got to protect it. People can't do something themselves, they want to tell you can't do it. You want something, go get it. Period."

Will Smith as Chris Gardner in the movie
The Pursuit of Happyness

When you think about offering support, what's the first thing you think of? Maybe it's financial support or emotional support. Maybe it's about encouraging someone by giving them words of affirmation. Or maybe it's something entirely different.

In her junior year of high school, Sophie butted heads with one of her teachers. This teacher was known for having no rubrics for grading papers or exams, and changing grades in the online system to help the students she liked best. In fact, in one instance, a student submitted the same exact paper twice and she received an 85 on the first one and a 100 on the second.

Sophie, who values fairness, had a tough time with this teacher and asked her parents for support in going to the school administration about the teacher. And sure, because they know Sophie, they knew she meant that she wanted them to have her back. To be ready to step in if something went wrong. But if Sophie had asked someone else (someone who didn't know her as well) for support in this situation, they may not have known what she meant.

Why? Because offering support can mean so many things, from empathizing and helping someone admit a vulnerability to raising the bar for them and shifting their perspective.

HELP STRATEGY 5
EMPATHIZE

Neil deGrasse Tyson said, "Humans aren't as good as we should be in our capacity to empathize with feelings and thoughts of others, be they humans or other animals on Earth. So maybe part of our formal education should be training in empathy. Imagine how different the world would be if, in fact, that were 'reading, writing, arithmetic, empathy.'"

Well, for today at least, Neil deGrasse Tyson's wish is coming true: you're about to get some formal education on empathy!

Let's start by defining some terms, especially the difference between sympathy and empathy. In general, "sympathy" is when you share the other person's feelings, whereas "empathy" is when you understand the feelings of another, but you don't necessarily feel them yourself.

In their book *Helping People Change: Coaching with Compassion for Lifelong Learning and Growth*, authors Ellen Van Oosten, Melvin Smith, and Richard E. Boyatzis describe three kinds of empathy:

1. **Cognitive**: conceptually understanding the other person's perspective

2. **Emotional**: being emotionally in tune with the other person

3. **Behavioral**: being motivated to help the other person in some way

When you're helping others by empathizing with them, you may be demonstrating one, two, or all three kinds.

Let's start with cognitive empathy—understanding the other person's perspective. Stephen Covey describes the skill set here as "listening with the intent to understand" (which also draws from Help Strategy #2: Listen to Learn). With empathic listening, you get inside your colleague, friend, or family member's frame of reference rather than using your own. You see the world through *their* eyes, rather than through yours. You imagine what it's like to be them in their situation, rather than think about what it would be like if *you* were in their situation. And the more you make it about you, the less likely you are to be helping them (unless the help they want is for you to share your own experience.)

As Harper Lee wrote in *To Kill a Mockingbird*: "You never really understand a person until you consider things from his point of view… Until you climb inside of his skin and walk around in it."

Of course, it can be easier to show cognitive empathy if you actually have been in a similar situation. But you run the risk of allowing biases to surface. For example, similarity bias—your unconscious preference for people who are like you—can drive you to empathize more with someone who, like you, has young children at home or a technical role you can relate to. In addition, your distance bias—an unconscious preference for things that happen closer in time or distance—can lead you to be more empathetic toward people who have situations you've also been through recently.

So be mindful that empathy isn't about you and your experience. It's about the person you're helping, and *their* experience.

Demonstrating cognitive empathy is also an important way to welcome diversity and be inclusive. Done effectively, it shows that you invite, appreciate, and respect someone else's experience and perspective—which may be very different from your own.

And it also requires you to develop your own help fluency, as you find that different people have different helping needs!

Unfortunately, you may think you're being empathetic when you're not. Here's an example of something that looks and sounds like empathy, but really isn't.

Your colleague: "Every time the client tries to move up the deadline, I get overwhelmed. I don't know how I can keep them happy without putting too much pressure on the team."

You: "I'm sure you'll figure it out. You always do."

While that might sound supportive, it's actually dismissive. And that is likely to make your team member feel unheard, and their challenge minimized. In other words, it's not helpful at all.

Here's an example of true cognitive empathy in action:

Your colleague: "Every time the client tries to move up the deadline, I get overwhelmed. I don't know how I can keep them happy without putting too much pressure on the team."

You: "That sounds stressful. I know how important being both client-focused and team-focused is for you."

You're demonstrating that you understand how they're thinking, and why they think it.

Let's move to emotional empathy—being emotionally in tune with the other person. This asks you to put yourself in the other person's *way of feeling*, not just in their *way of thinking*. And unlike sympathy, you don't have to feel what they feel. You can recognize differences while also recognizing that however they feel is valid—and you're not trying to change it.

Here's an example of helpful emotional empathy:

Your colleague: "Every time the client tries to move up the deadline, I get overwhelmed. I don't know how I can keep them happy without putting too much pressure on the team."

You: "I'm sorry you're dealing with that. I can hear that you're overwhelmed, and maybe also frustrated and concerned. Did I get that right?"

Now compare that to another way that's less helpful (and also more common):

Your colleague: "Every time the client tries to move up the deadline, I get overwhelmed. I don't know how I can keep them happy without putting too much pressure on the team."

You: "Ugh! That's the worst! I hate when that happens. When I had to deal with that, I was frustrated all the time. So what happened to me was…"

Sound familiar? And while that might sound empathetic, it's actually less about their feelings and more about your feelings. It's less about exploring and welcoming differences and more about you sharing what's the same. And that is likely to make your colleague feel like it's all about you, not them.

Finally, let's examine behavioral empathy, which is when your cognitive empathy (understanding their perspective) and emotional empathy (recognizing their feelings) combine to motivate you to want to offer even more help. And "even more help" doesn't mean telling them what to do, or fixing it for them—unless that's the help they want and need.

Here's an example of how to be helpful:

Your colleague: "Every time the client tries to move up the deadline, I get overwhelmed. I don't know how I can keep them happy without putting too much pressure on the team."

You: "That does sound overwhelming. What kind of help would be most useful to you? I can help you brainstorm some new options, or just listen while you vent, or share my experience... or something else."

Now compare that to how we typically try to help:

Your colleague: "Every time the client tries to move up the deadline, I get overwhelmed. I don't know how I can keep them happy without putting too much pressure on the team."

You: "You know what? Let me talk to the client. Leave it to me."

While "leave it to me" might sound helpful, it won't help your colleague develop new awareness, skills, or strategies. "Leave it to me" means you'll do it your way, instead of helping your team member to develop "their way." You'll end up needing to intervene every single time.

Now imagine saying "leave it to me" not just with your coworkers, but with your family members, and friends. That kind of help costs you your own time and energy.

In fact, you don't even need to speak to empathize. Sometimes your silence is more powerful than any words you could say. While you may feel the urge to say something, maybe because you feel uncomfortable with an awkward silence, resist that urge. Hold space for someone to cry, talk, think, or sit silently, and you may be surprised at how much better that actually makes them feel.

When Deb's mother-in-law Joan passed away, her entire family was grieving the loss. Every single day for several months after her death, Deb's husband Mike and his two siblings Jon and Debby called their dad Archie to see how he was doing. They would talk about everything from their feelings of shock and sadness to legal documents that needed to be reviewed, and thank you notes that needed to be sent.

And every single day, Deb also called Archie, but it was a different kind of conversation. While Archie knew that she was grieving as well, as an in-law (or an "outlaw" as he affectionately called her) she was one degree removed from the pain of losing a parent. He didn't want to compound his children's suffering with his suffering. So Deb just held space for him to cry. She never told him that it was going to be OK. She never said that he would feel better soon. She never told him how lucky he was to have had such a long and loving marriage. She sat with him in silence, not pretending to understand the magnitude of the loss he was dealing with. She just gave him the space he needed to grieve. This was how she empathized with him.

Empathizing doesn't require you to say anything, and it also doesn't require you to agree with the other person. But it does require that you connect cognitively (by understanding their situation), emotionally (by recognizing their emotions), and behaviorally (by showing them support).

HELP STRATEGY ⑥
INVITE THEM TO ADMIT SOMETHING VULNERABLE

"Brave doesn't mean you're not scared. It means you go on even though you're scared."

Angie Thomas, *The Hate U Give*

Sometimes, your colleague, friend, or family member might just need a place where they can talk about something that feels hard for them to share. They need a space for them to admit how they may have contributed to a problem, or made a mistake, or to talk about something that feels scary or personal.

When Sophie was in 7th grade, she had done some research about the anxiety she was experiencing. She diagnosed herself with obsessive compulsive disorder, which was later confirmed by a psychiatrist. But despite feeling confident in her self-diagnosis, she was nervous to share this personal and frightening information. She knew, however, that if she didn't tell anyone, she wasn't going to get the help she needed. Sophie decided to tell her mom Deb about her self-diagnosis, who immediately helped her get support and treatment. Why did Sophie choose Deb? Because Deb had a solid track record of letting Sophie know that she could tell her anything safely.

You may sense that your coworker is having a hard time managing a new baby and a new boss at the same time, but you're not sure how to invite that conversation without prying. You may intuit that your friend is having money challenges but you don't want to embarrass her. Or you may just feel like something is bothering someone you care about, but you're not sure what—and you don't want to just let it linger.

Here are five ways to invite someone to admit something vulnerable:

- "I want to talk to you about something that feels a little awkward... but I am going to embrace the awkward and go for it because you're important to me."

- "I want to ask you about something—and I'm not upset with you. I promise!"

- "You've been on my mind a lot lately, and I would like to share why..."

- "I'd like to talk to you about how you're doing/feeling because I care about you. I'm feeling concerned, and I'd like to help. Would you be open to a conversation?"

- "You haven't seemed like yourself for a little while, and I'd like to check in for a few minutes. Is now a good time?"

The worst that can happen is that you miscalculated and they were fine, or they don't want to talk about it, or they get annoyed that you overstepped. In any of those cases, you can just say some version of "Message received!" and move on. The best that can happen is that you offer the right kind of help at exactly the right time.

And no matter what happens, keep in mind that this helping strategy is only as helpful as your commitment to really hear the other person without judgment, keep the conversation confidential (unless you've asked for permission to share or they're at risk of harming themselves or others), and make it clear that you appreciate that they were willing to share their challenges with you.

HELP STRATEGY 7
HELP THEM TOLERATE DISCOMFORT AND AMBIGUITY

When Sophie and Deb wrote their first book together, *Overcoming Overthinking: 36 Ways to Tame Anxiety for Work, School, and Life*, they shared a strategy called "Meet Them Before You Move Them." The idea is that we often feel uncomfortable when someone else is feeling uncomfortable, so we try to cheer them up, or offer them a bright side to consider, or distract them from their discomfort. In other words, we try to *move them* away from their pain rather than *meeting them* where they are.

Think about Tom Hanks as Rockford Peaches baseball manager Jimmy Dugan in the movie *A League of Their Own* yelling, "There's no crying in baseball!" to a player who was in tears. He was trying to *move her* rather than *meet her.*

Here's what it can look like in real life: Imagine your colleague is frustrated with feedback from their boss. You might say something like: "At least you didn't get fired!" or "You know he sets impossible standards!" Your intention is to make them feel better—to move them from their frustration and disappointment to something more positive. But the impact may be that they don't have a chance to experience their emotions, and seek to understand what those feelings are telling them about what matters to them.

In situations where a colleague, friend, or family member feels mad, sad, or bad in some way, stay away from what's known as "toxic positivity." Toxic positivity is the belief that people should maintain a positive attitude and mindset no matter how challenging their situation is. What's wrong with this? It invalidates the other person's emotional and practical experience, and judges them for how they are handling their pain. What makes toxic positivity so egregious is that it is likely to lead to secondary negative emotions: your colleague now feels ashamed of being frustrated or embarrassed about being disappointed.

Whitney Goodman LMFT from The Collaborative Counseling Center LLC shares these toxic positivity phrases to avoid:

- "Everything happens for a reason."
- "You'll bounce back—you always do."
- "Think positive!"
- "Don't stress about this!"
- "You just need to try harder."
- "There are so many people that have it worse than you."
- "What doesn't kill us makes us stronger."
- "This too shall pass."

Unless our colleague or friend has asked to be cheered up, distracted, or given a silver lining, we're not helping them by using any of these phrases. We're just helping ourselves feel better.

When you avoid using toxic positivity, you are showing the other person that your goal isn't to move them, but it really is to meet them exactly where they are.

Here are some helpful alternatives:

- "Thank you for confiding in me."
- "This is hard."
- "I believe you."
- "And how else are you feeling?"
- "I am here to support you through this."
- "What would be most helpful to you right now?"
- "I've been through something similar. And while I don't want to make this about me, I am open to sharing my experience with you if and when it would be helpful."

You become a sophisticated helper when you can learn to tolerate someone else's discomfort in service of them. You can remind yourself that you've survived 100% of the times when you felt uncomfortable or unsure, and if someone's coming to you for help, the conversation is about them, not you.

HELP STRATEGY 8

SUMMON THEIR STRENGTHS

Mahatma Gandhi said, "Man often becomes what he believes himself to be. If I keep on saying to myself that I cannot do a certain thing, it is possible that I may end up really becoming incapable of doing it. On the contrary, if I have the belief that I can do it, I shall surely acquire the capacity to do it even if I may not have it at the beginning."

And of course, that's true for all genders.

Every single one of us has experienced a loss of confidence. You might have made a decision that didn't turn out well, and so you forget that you really do have good judgment. Or you had a difficult interaction with a colleague, leading you to wonder if you really are a team-player after all. Or maybe you made a careless mistake, and thought to yourself, *Maybe I'm not as detail-oriented as I always thought I was.*

We hope that you had someone in your life who helped remind you of your strengths in those moments. And if you did, you had someone who was using an important helping skill: summoning your strengths.

Research by the VIA Institute on Character shows that when we remind someone of their strengths, we can help boost their confidence, increase their happiness, strengthen relationships, manage problems, reduce stress, accomplish goals, build meaning and purpose, and improve their performance.

And who wouldn't want that?

It's an encouraging way of reminding someone who they are, what they're capable of, and what you and others value in them—in the best of times and in the worst of times.

Deb's client Ellie called her with a tricky situation: as the new executive director of a small private school, she needed to suspend one of her students for violating the school's drug use policy. What made this particularly challenging was that this student's parents were the largest donors to the school. In the past, these parents had asked for rules to be bent for their kids in the school, intimating that there was a direct correlation between their philanthropic giving and rule-bending.

Ellie did not need Deb to tell her what to do. Ellie did not want Deb to step in and fix it for her. In fact, Ellie wasn't sure what she needed at all. So Deb empathized with the difficulty of her situation, and then took a moment to summon one of Ellie's strengths:

"Ellie, one of your greatest assets is your integrity. You have an exceptional track record of doing the thing that is right and healthy—personally, professionally, and organizationally. Do you see that about yourself too?"

Ellie did. And being reminded that she had a core strength with an impressive success rate that she could leverage in this situation was all that she needed to decide how to move forward.

Ellie, like most of us, just needed to be reminded of her strengths, especially when she was feeling unsure, or unprepared.

And sometimes, reminding someone of who they are at their best can be as simple as this exchange from the movie *Shrek*, about an ogre and a beautiful princess Fiona, who is placed under a curse that transforms her into an ogre at night.

Princess Fiona: "I'm supposed to be beautiful."

Shrek: "But you are beautiful."

Letting someone know that you see their unique kind of beauty, inside or outside, could be just the help that someone needs.

Consider one of your colleagues, friends, or family members whom you think could use a little support. What is something spectacular you see in them that they may need to be reminded about?

Here are some strengths to get you started:

Authenticity	Hopefulness
Bravery	Humility
Caring	Humor
Compassion	Integrity
Creativity	Kindness
Curiosity	Logic
Dedication	Loyalty
Determination	Open-mindedness
Discipline	Passion
Enthusiasm	Patience
Fairness	Prudence
Forgiveness	Resilience
Generosity	Strategic
Gratitude	Trustworthiness
Honesty	Versatility

And while you're in the process of identifying someone else's strengths, don't forget to highlight the strengths you see in yourself.

HELP STRATEGY ⑨
RAISE THE BAR FOR THEM

"Why, sometimes, I've believed as many as six impossible things before breakfast."

Lewis Carroll, *Through the Looking-Glass*

Hopefully, you've had people in your life—parents, teachers, coaches, bosses—who have brought out the best in you—encouraging and inspiring you to do more than you thought you could. Yes, even things that seemed impossible.

And you've also likely had people in your life who have done the complete opposite, leading you to feel disengaged, discouraged, and disappointed—in them, and in yourself.

Chances are, you want to be the first type of helper, right?

So, what separates those friends, family members, and colleagues who help others achieve more from those who contribute to self-doubt?

Raising the bar higher for them than they might for themselves, challenging them to do something they didn't think they could do, or pushing them to complete a task that feels hard or scary.

Doctors, behavioral scientists, and educators have known for decades that our expectations of another person can influence their behavior—for better or for worse.

In 1968, Robert Rosenthal and Lenore Jacobson conducted a study in which they discovered that teachers with high expectations for particular students provided those students with more support and encouragement, more challenging material to learn, more feedback, and more opportunity to speak in discussions. This led to a significantly higher performance in these students, compared to those teachers who had low expectations for another group of students. As a result of these low expectations, they pulled back on resources, support, and feedback, yielding less successful outcomes.

This phenomenon is known as a "self-fulfilling prophecy" or the Pygmalion Effect— which you may have heard of. Pygmalion was a sculptor in Greek mythology who, by his sheer effort and will, brought a statue to life. And it has been replicated time and time again over the decades, in family homes, courtrooms, military training centers, and in businesses.

Research on the Pygmalion Effect has continuously shown that our expectations of others impact their performance. We know that if we raise the bar for someone by raising our expectations, it is likely that this will enhance their performance, whether it's a score on an exam, a performance review from a manager, or committing to a healthier habit.

When Deb first joined a CrossFit gym, she was intimidated by the other people working out around her. They ranged from firefighters and police officers to mixed martial arts competitors and military veterans. She didn't notice too many other leadership coaches and speakers in the mix! She also noticed that she was lifting the lightest weights, running the slowest pace (if you could even call what she was doing "running"), and taking more water breaks than anyone else.

And yet, her instructors called her a name that immediately communicated their expectations of her. And that name was "athlete." By telling Deb that she was an athlete from Day 1, and giving her the same label as everyone else in the group, her coaches helped her feel like she belonged there. Even though Deb didn't see herself as an athlete *yet*, she realized that by her coaches raising the bar for her, she would soon be able to raise the bar—literally and figuratively—for herself.

In the world of wellness, we know that we are best helped by people who can see a future version of ourselves that is healthier than we can envision. And in the world of work, leaders who have been found to be positive "Pygmalions" are usually also the best managers. Unfortunately, research shows that most managers are more effective in communicating low expectations to their direct reports than in communicating high expectations.

So when should you raise the bar for someone? When they are:

Reluctant to raise their own expectations and standards. For example, your best friend tells you that she is staying in her current relationship because she doesn't think she will meet someone who shares her interests, and who would be understanding that she has a son with special needs, and who would support her successful career. You might say, "I believe you deserve to have all of those things in a relationship. And I'm here to remind you that you shouldn't settle for anyone who doesn't embrace all of you."

Resistant to engage in a process that will help them get what they want. Maybe your son wants to raise his GPA so that he can have a wider range of choices when applying to college. However, he doesn't want to get the tutoring in history and science that would really help him bridge the gap. You might offer, "I want you to have every option possible for you when you apply to college. I am certain that if you put in the work now, you'll transform your GPA. And I have no doubt in your ability to do hard things."

Ruminating about whether or not to do something that matters to them. Imagine that your partner keeps going back and forth about whether to apply for an open management position at her company, even though she has repeatedly expressed an interest in advancing her career. You could try something like: "I see that you're having a tough time making a decision here. And while I will support you no matter what you choose, let me just say that I believe this role was made for you. You bring the knowledge, skills, and experience they want—and then some!"

Ready but unmotivated because the challenge feels uncomfortable or overwhelming. Maybe your friend shared with you that they feel like they aren't being social enough, but they don't feel motivated to invite their other friends to go out. You can raise the bar for them by pushing their comfort level to the edge—but not over it. You may say something like this: "I want you to invite one of your friends for a dinner date or a walk, and the next time we talk, I want you to tell me about it." Or you can say something like this: "If you invite someone to go out with you this week, I will also do something I'm not motivated to do (exercise, call my uncle, write an overdue article, etc.)." Being an accountability partner for your friends and colleagues can encourage and motivate them to challenge themselves.

It's clear that your mindsets, your words, and your behaviors matter when you truly want to motivate others to do—and be—their best. As chef, entrepreneur, and author David Chang put it, "If people think you are this amazing, own it." And raising the bar for them, when they haven't for themselves, may be the best gift of help you can give them—to help them see it and own it.

HELP STRATEGY 🔟
HELP THEM FOCUS ON WHAT IS WORKING

You probably don't see a problem and think to yourself, *I wonder what's going **right** here.* Instead, you might think, *What did I do wrong? What do I need to fix?*

You can support someone by offering to help them look at what's going *right* instead of what's going wrong. Or, more accurately, you can help them see what's going right *as well* as what's going wrong.

This employs a foundational approach that Deb learned when she performed improvisational comedy as an undergraduate at The University of Michigan: "yes, and..." In improvisation, saying "yes, and..." helps the performers remember to accept what another participant has stated ("yes") and then expand on that line of thinking ("and").

It's much more accepting, supportive, and helpful than saying "yes, but..." "But" negates the other person's perspective, shuts down the lines of communication, and can have a judgmental impact.

When your father says to you, "I have been having trouble remembering things," you might say, "Yes, *and* today seems like a better day than yesterday for you."

When your boss says, "The client's changing demands are driving me bananas," you could respond with, "Yes, *and* you don't have to deal with it alone. How can we help?"

When your friend says, "I haven't had a full night's sleep in months," you might say, "Yes, *and* the baby is just starting to sleep through the night. You're just days away from getting six solid hours."

But before you use this helping strategy, don't forget to ask them if they'd like to examine their situation from another perspective. If you're trying to cheer them up when they're not ready for that, or you're attempting to make yourself more comfortable with your friend or colleague's discomfort, re-read the previous section on "toxic positivity."

Sophie has had straight A's through high school and her first year of college. When she received a 78 on an exam her sophomore year of college, she was surprised by two things: the grade and her reaction. If Sophie had gotten a 78 in high school, she would have protested, cried, and moped around for days. This time, Sophie was proud of herself. "This is 78% more than I would have known three weeks ago. I've learned a ton!" she told Deb, who had expected Sophie to be in tears.

Sophie was proud that she wasn't afraid to ask her professor to explain where she went wrong. She also moved on from the very momentary disappointment and focused on what she could do to prepare for the next exam.

If someone else had told Sophie that she should be proud of her hard work, that she did well, or that she should be happy she didn't fail, Sophie would have been frustrated. These are only helpful things to say when you say them to *yourself*. However, even though you shouldn't say these things to someone else, you can ask them questions to help them focus on what is working.

Here are some questions you can ask to help someone shift their focus from what isn't going well to what is:

"Where is the problem not?"

"What isn't keeping you up at night these days?"

"If you had to name 2% of your work or life that's going well, what would it be?"

"Where do you see a glimmer of hope?"

"Where do you get your energy from?"

"What did you do absolutely right in this situation?"

"What are you most proud of about yourself right now?"

"What are you grateful for?"

As J.R.R. Tolkien wrote in *The Two Towers*: "There is some good in this world, and it's worth fighting for."

Supporting your colleagues, friends, and family members comes in many forms—from listening and asking powerful questions to empathizing and summoning strengths. Learning how to provide, ask for, and accept support is critical for all of us to get through life. As *Project Runway* star and producer Tim Gunn remarked, "Life is not a solo act. It's a huge collaboration, and we all need to assemble around us the people who care about us, and support us in times of strife."

CHAPTER 8: REVIEW AND REFLECT

 REVIEW:

- Empathizing with others doesn't require you to sympathize with them or agree with them. You just need to be willing to understand how they think and how they feel, and be interested in helping them.

- When someone is sharing difficult emotions, avoid using "toxic positivity" to try to cheer them up or to relieve yourself of discomfort. Be willing to sit with them as they experience pain or ambiguity.

- To help someone who is experiencing a loss of confidence, remind them of the strengths that you and others see in them.

REFLECT:

- Who is someone at work or in your personal life who is going through a difficult time? How can you do a better job of being with them where they are emotionally, rather than trying to cheer them up or push them to see the bright side?

- What is a tough emotion you're dealing with right now? Who do you know who can empathize with you without trying to change you, cheer you up prematurely, or make it about them and their experience?

CHAPTER 9:

GIVE DIRECTION

"My name is Harvey Milk, and I'm here to recruit you.

I want to recruit you for the fight to preserve your democracy.

Brothers and sisters, you must come out.

Come out to your parents.

Come out to your friends, if indeed they are your friends.

Come out to your neighbors. Come out to your fellow workers.

Once and for all, let's break down the myths, and destroy the lies and distortions—for your sake, for their sake, for the sake of all the youngsters who have been scared by the votes from Dade to Eugene."

Sean Penn as Harvey Milk, the first openly gay elected official in the history of California, from the movie *Milk*

If you're trying to help someone who is stuck, who doesn't know how to move forward, who doesn't have the necessary experience, who isn't sure what support they have—or when you are deeply committed to there being one single, best way to get something done—give them direction.

But as simple as that might sound, it's still multifaceted. Direction may mean just telling them what to do. And it can also look like taking something off their plate that they just can't handle right now, doing it with them, teaching them how, making recommendations, or offering resources.

HELP STRATEGY **11**
TELL THEM WHAT TO DO

In Chapter 2, you read about some key indicators that you might need to be directive to be helpful. If the other person lacks the necessary knowledge, skill, or experience to do this task, tell them what to do. If they don't need to learn how to do it for the future, tell them what to do. When you need something done immediately, tell them what to do. When you don't have the time to commit yourself to their development, tell them what to do. If you believe that there's a right way and a wrong way, don't make them try to figure it out—tell them what to do.

Far too often, Deb hears the leaders she works with describe that they themselves are trying to "coach" an employee to come to the "right" conclusion. However, if the leader is already committed to a particular outcome and they haven't shared that with their direct report, they're not coaching. They're manipulating.

Whether you want to help your child by telling them how to greet their friend's parents when they meet them for the first time, or help your new coworker by telling them how to use their key card for entry to the building, telling them what to do can speed things up and minimize misunderstandings and mistakes.

And also keep in mind that repeatedly and consistently telling people what to do can undermine their autonomy, confidence, competence, and development. So use it sparingly!

HELP STRATEGY ⏺12
TAKE SOMETHING OFF THEIR PLATE

"Do, or do not. There is no 'try.'"

Yoda

It can often be easier to take something off someone's plate than to help them understand either why they can't do it, or how they can do it themselves. And while this isn't a solution to every problem, it can be a solution to challenges that need to be handled immediately.

Taking a project or task off someone's plate can also free them up to focus on more pressing tasks or higher priority items. In fact, The Mayo Clinic cites offloading non-essential tasks to non-physician staff as a successful intervention to prevent physician burnout.

If you're looking to create a culture of helping in your department or in your family, asking "What can I take off your plate?" regularly is a powerful way to send the message that helping out is the way we operate around here.

It's also important to remember that taking something off someone's plate shouldn't be done with strings attached, or as a quid pro quo, or so that you can bring it up to them later to evoke feelings of guilt, shame, or obligation. If you can't take something off someone's plate without needing to remind them that you helped them, don't offer.

One other tip: consider a "plate exchange" where you trade tasks with someone else. If you do the cooking and your partner does the dishes after, you're already doing it. If there's a task that's challenging, boring, or demotivating to you (that you don't need to get better at), swap it with someone who finds that task more tolerable. Deb's husband Michael is in charge of all business and household paperwork, since paperwork gives Deb what she calls "emotional hives." In exchange, Deb arranges all of the family's travel, whether for business or pleasure.

Whether you take something off someone's plate completely, or do a plate exchange, know that you're helping someone else take control of their workload and headspace.

HELP STRATEGY 13
DO IT WITH THEM, SIDE BY SIDE

Let's say your kid needs help with their math homework (and you better hope that they haven't changed math that much since you took it). Instead of solving the problems for them, you can do the problems together, step by step. Sometimes, this kind of help allows someone who is feeling overwhelmed (whether it's with math problems, personal finances, or anything else) to break down the problem into smaller steps. This allows them to focus on one thing at a time as opposed to being overwhelmed with fixing everything at once.

As a TA, Sophie often uses this strategy to help her students. She knows she can't tell them how to do it, nor would it be a good use of time for her to tell her students that they need to pay more attention during the lecture. So, she walks them through the problems step by step.

"I don't know how to do this," her students often tell her.

"Let's just focus on the first step," Sophie responds.

Sophie often realizes that her students are just stuck on one small part of the problem, but they actually know how to do the rest. When she works with them one step at a time, they realize this, too, and feel more confident moving forward.

Another example might look like this:

If you are having trouble staying motivated to do your scheduled workouts, you might need someone to do the workouts with you. You don't need them to teach you how to work out (you already know how), but them doing it with you helps hold you accountable for your commitments.

Take a minute to think about a problem you've had in the past few months. If you want to figure out what kind of direction you need (if any), ask yourself these questions:

- Will I be OK if this is not solved immediately?
- Do I have the capacity/time to fix this?
- Do I know how to do any part of this?
- Is this a skill I will need to learn in the future?

If you answered yes to these questions, it's likely that you need someone to walk you through this step by step. If you answered no, you might want someone to take this off of your plate. And if you had mixed answers, that's OK too! You may need someone to take part of it off your plate, do it with you step by step for part, or you may want to look at the other help strategies to figure out what would be best for you.

HELP STRATEGY ⑭
TEACH THEM HOW TO DO SOMETHING

"Steal as much wisdom from other people as you can."
Comedian and writer Aziz Ansari

Teaching someone how to approach and master a task or skill is an ideal helping method when it's a skill they want to be able to have in the future, when they've never done it before or want to do it better, and when you know how to do it yourself.

When Deb's clients ask her for help in developing a presentation for a meeting or a conference, she doesn't say, "Send me the background and I'll write it for you." She teaches her clients how to build a presentation from a blank page so that they can do it themselves in the future—and without her.

Now here's the tricky part: Teaching someone how to do something that you know how to do well isn't necessarily an intuitive skill. Baseball legend Ted Williams was notorious for being a brilliant player but a terrible coach. Why? Because he couldn't cope with the fact that his players weren't as talented as he was. He didn't learn to adjust his style to help players who were, as Senators star Frank Howard remarked, "mere mortals."

If you're planning to teach someone how to do something, you may need to ask for help for yourself on some teaching skills!

HELP STRATEGY ⑮
RECOMMEND AN APPROACH TO TRY

Picture this: your close friend calls you and explains that it's time for him to discuss the topic of "consent" with his teenager, but he doesn't know how to approach it without making the conversation feel uncomfortable. He knows that it's the right time for this conversation, but he is unsure of the *how*.

You might ask: "Would you like me to suggest an approach?"

Assuming that he says, "Yes! Thank you!" you might suggest that he has the conversation in stages so that it doesn't feel overwhelming to him or his teen. Or maybe you suggest that he approaches his teen like an adult, so that his child feels respected and trusted. Or maybe you recommend he start the conversation by asking his teen what they already know about the topic.

Recommending an approach can feel less pushy than telling someone exactly how to handle a problem. And that's partially because of the language we use.

Say, "You may want to consider doing X," instead of "You should do X." Say "I want to give you a recommendation that you can take or leave," instead of "I'm going to tell you what you need to do." You want to be gentle and thoughtful, not aggressive and commanding. Think of it like holding out a dessert platter and inviting someone to take the offerings they'd like to try, rather than putting a piece of strawberry cheesecake on their plate.

Sophie uses this help strategy with her brother Jake when he's trying to figure out how to convince their parents to get him something. For example, when Jake wanted an Xbox, he asked Sophie how he should ask their parents for it. She recommended, "You may want to reconsider using 'everyone else has one' as a reason for getting one. Mom and Dad don't care what everyone else is doing." She also suggested that he consider offering to contribute to the cost of the Xbox. Recommending this approach gave Jake the flexibility to decline or make his own decision, allowed him to consider his options without feeling pressured, and ultimately led to Jake getting an Xbox.

HELP STRATEGY 16
RECOMMEND WHAT TO AVOID

Advising isn't just about helping someone figure out what to do, but also what **not** to do.

For example, when the COVID-19 pandemic started, the CDC recommended that we avoid touching our faces and gathering in groups. Identifying what to avoid, not just what to do (wash our hands, get tested, quarantine, etc.), saved countless lives. We often underestimate the power of someone recommending what to avoid doing partially because we like advice that promotes action, not inaction.

When helping your coworker prepare for an important client pitch, you might suggest they avoid making small talk if you know that this client likes to get down to business. If you're helping your mom have a calm conversation with your sister, you might suggest she avoid bringing up the fact that she went to her in-laws for the holidays two years in a row. Many of Deb's clients ask her, "How do I tell an employee that they're being defensive?" Deb's recommendation? "Avoid calling them 'defensive'. If they're not already defensive, calling them defensive can make them defensive! Instead, describe the behaviors you observe, such as them arguing with feedback, that you'd like to see them change."

If you have the inside scoop on what someone should avoid in terms of timing, tone, technique, or anything else, sharing it can be incredibly helpful.

HELP STRATEGY ⑰
OFFER RESOURCES

There will be times when someone will ask you for your help or advice, and you will be stumped. While you have a depth and breadth of knowledge about a wide range of topics, for *this* particular subject, you're coming up empty. Or maybe, you do have some knowledge, but you're swamped, and can't free yourself up to help directly. Perhaps it's a topic where you could provide a good enough answer, but not a great one. And maybe it's a scenario where the highest and best use of your expertise isn't for explaining the fundamentals, but for the more nuanced parts of an issue.

In any of those scenarios, offer resources that aren't *you*.

Let's say your friend is looking for a new job, and since you've recently started a new one yourself, she asks you for help preparing for her interview. Yes, you could help her, but since you've just started your new position at work, you don't have a lot of free time.

Instead, explain that to her, and send her a link to a few articles, videos, or podcasts by experts in the field that will prepare her as well as you could, if not better. Or connect her to the coach you worked with who helped you get ready for your own job interview.

Let's say your coworker is overwhelmed with parenting one-year-old twins who aren't sleeping through the night. He asks you how you managed. He asks you what to do. He tells you why what you're suggesting won't work for *his* kids. He does this every single day.

You know what it's time for? Resources that aren't you!!

Tell him that you've shared all that you personally know that would be helpful. And suggest he check in with the sleep guru you used, or the book you read, or whatever might help him move forward that doesn't involve *you*.

In the leadership development programs that Deb designs and delivers for clients, she always includes "self-directed resources" as part of the curriculum. Whether these are articles about how to give effective feedback, podcasts on navigating change, or TED Talks on a range of topics, these "booster shots" of information give participants the opportunity to engage in self-directed learning in their own time. And it means that Deb doesn't have to be an expert on everything (phew!), but she can connect leaders to experts who can supplement her own knowledge and experience.

Whether you're low on time, expertise, personal experience, patience—or it just seems like the best way to help this particular person to help themselves—connecting them with resources may be just what the doctor ordered. You don't have to know everything yourself to be a good helper.

And, like with any other helping strategy, there's a caveat: Be careful when sending unsolicited resources to other people.

You probably know someone who constantly sends you articles, videos, or other resources on topics like "How to Lose Ten Pounds in a Month," or "How to Get your Kids to stop Talking Back," or "How to Know that You're in a Go-Nowhere Job" (and maybe you're that person). And sure, it's likely that this person is trying to be helpful. But the truth is, when these resources arrive without invitation or warning, they can feel like criticism.

When Deb's friend Sadie adopted a baby, Fiona, who had Down Syndrome, Sadie made it as clear as she possibly could to friends and family that she and her wife Lucy didn't want or need advice. Nevertheless, Sadie and Lucy's parents, friends, and coworkers flooded them with resources: articles about how to raise a child with Down Syndrome, suggestions for medical experts (many of whom had nothing to do with Down Syndrome), "inspirational" stories about children with Down Syndrome who had grown up to live happy, healthy, productive, and independent lives, and more.

Not a single one of these resources felt helpful to Sadie and Lucy—despite the senders' good intentions. These suggestions felt invasive, judgmental, and critical. Sadie and Lucy interpreted these resources as other people's concerns that they couldn't handle Fiona's challenges on their own, or that they weren't being thorough in their approach.

This flood of resources also meant that, in addition to raising a child with special needs, Lucy and Sadie had to put time and energy into "thanking" people for sending resources they didn't want or need. They also had to keep telling well-meaning friends and family that they had it handled, while wrestling with the feeling that other people seemed to think they didn't know what they were doing.

If you're going to send someone a resource, ask them:

"Would it be helpful for me to send you _____?"

If they say yes, go for it.

If they say no, let it go.

HELP STRATEGY ⓲
SHARE YOUR OWN EXPERIENCE

When it comes to talking openly and honestly about mental health, Sophie and Deb often share their own experiences with others as a way to help other people. Sharing your own experience can help someone else feel less alone, more understood, and motivate or encourage them to keep pushing through whatever is holding them back.

For Sophie, sharing her own experience often involves talking about her four mental illnesses: generalized anxiety disorder, panic disorder, obsessive-compulsive disorder, and trichotillomania (a compulsive hair-pulling disorder). She shared her story about these in her book *Don't Tell Me to Relax!: One Teen's Journey to Survive Anxiety (and How You Can Too)*, and also receives frequent emails from teens asking her for advice. Sophie is not a licensed psychologist, but she is able to help a lot of kids and teens deal with mental illness by sharing how she struggled, reached out for help, and how she copes.

When coaches who are new to the field call Deb, they are interested in hearing about Deb's experience building a coaching business, the mistakes she's made, and tips that she has based on her years of experience in the field.

Your experience doesn't need to be life-changing to be worthy of sharing. Maybe you had a fight with your partner, and you share with a friend how you learned to forgive each other. Maybe you quit your job without having a backup plan, and you share with a colleague how you dealt with that uncertainty. You've had a lifetime's worth of experiences, both good and bad, that are worth sharing with others because it's possible that your experience is exactly what someone else needs to hear in order to move forward.

And, it goes without saying (but the authors are going to say it anyway): Ask before offering: "Would it be helpful for me to share my experience with you... or are you looking for something else?"

CHAPTER 9: REVIEW AND REFLECT

 REVIEW:

- When someone doesn't have experience or skill in getting a task done, offering them concrete and clear direction may be the best way to help them.

- Teach someone how to do something that they'll need to do again in the future. If they don't need to learn it and/or they won't need to do it again, consider helping them by taking this task off their plate.

- Share your own experience with others who may be in a similar situation to one you faced—but make sure that they *want* to hear about how you handled it before telling them how you did it.

REFLECT:

- Who in your work or life could use some advice, recommendations, or direction? And how can you make sure that this is what *they* want and need rather than what you know how to do best to be helpful?

- What is a challenge you're facing right now where you could use someone to step in and share their expertise or experience? Who will you ask to do that?

CHAPTER 10:

PLAN AND EXECUTE

Getting things done takes determination and drive, concentration and commitment, energy and engagement. It also takes clarity, direction, and focus. To plan and execute on any task—whether it's launching a new business or preparing for the middle school science fair—you need a goal.

And the people you live with and work with are no exception. So be prepared to help them plan and execute on their goals.

They, and you, will be in very good company.

In 1961, President John F. Kennedy said, "I believe this nation should commit itself to achieving the goal, before the decade is out, of landing a man on the moon and returning him safely to Earth." He did it—and he didn't do it without help.

Oprah Winfrey's goal was to help people take better control of their life and destiny. She did it—and she didn't do it without help, either.

But goal setting doesn't have to be as enormous or momentous as space travel or producing and hosting an award-winning talk show. Your friend may want to be able to lift 40 lbs. over her head in preparation for an upcoming backpacking trip, or your business partner might want to multiply your revenue 1.5x so that you can hire additional staff.

And whether you're trying to help your colleague, friend, or family member achieve something big or small, helping them set goals is an important part of the process.

As *Studying Smart* author Diana Scharf-Hunt wrote, "Goals are dreams with deadlines."

HELP STRATEGY ⓳
SET S.M.A.R.T. AND S.M.A.R.T.E.S.T. GOALS

Research on goal setting shows that it can focus our attention on the most important priorities, mobilize our efforts in proportion to the demands of the task, develop persistence and tenacity, support us in overcoming procrastination, ensure accountability and productivity, and much more.

That's a pretty significant list of benefits!

So, what's your role in helping others set goals? It's to support them in developing S.M.A.R.T. and S.M.A.R.T.E.S.T. goals.

Let's start with S.M.A.R.T. goals. You may already know this acronym very well, but here's a refresher. S.M.A.R.T. stands for:

Specific, **M**easurable, **A**ttainable, **R**elevant, **T**ime-Bound

S.M.A.R.T. goals help others to clarify their objectives and bring them closer to reality.

S.M.A.R.T. goals are focused, create verifiable milestones, and give an estimation of the goal's attainability.

S.M.A.R.T. goal setting is a well-known and established tool to help people plan and achieve goals. It's what transforms good intentions into actions.

And yes, sometimes we may want to upgrade our help (and their outcomes) even more. This is when you can support someone who may already have S.M.A.R.T. goals (but still may be stuck or feel unmotivated) with the S.M.A.R.T.E.S.T. ones.

How do you help them make goals the S.M.A.R.T.E.S.T.?

By pressing them to consider the following:

Special: "What makes this unique or important to you?"

Motivating: "What are you looking forward to most?"

Aspirational: "What will be different for you when you achieve this?"

Resonant: "How does this goal align with your values?"

Timely: "What makes now the right time for you to take this on?"

Energizing: "Where's your energy for doing this coming from?"

Simple: "How can you simplify this?"

Truthful: "How will you trust yourself in the process?"

Adding a S.M.A.R.T.E.S.T. perspective to a S.M.A.R.T. goal can move it from someone's hands and head to include their heart as well.

Deb knows this firsthand. After more than 40 years of setting S.M.A.R.T. goals that were related to weight loss ("I want to lose

20 lbs. before the first day of school," "I want to be two sizes smaller by my wedding," "I want to lose 70 lbs. by 12 months after my babies are born"), Deb was done. She had achieved all of those S.M.A.R.T. goals, and yet, none of those outcomes were permanent, or even as satisfying as she'd hoped. She found herself in a seemingly endless cycle of weight loss and weight gain, of celebration and shame, of obsessive thinking and compulsive measuring, and ultimately feared that her body image would never recover.

So, she decided to try something new—a S.M.A.R.T. and S.M.A.R.T.E.S.T. approach. She reached out to an expert in intuitive eating, which promotes a healthy attitude toward food and body image, and asked for help.

Her goals were S.M.A.R.T. Specifically, Deb wanted to stop thinking about calorie intake every single time she took a bite or sip. She would measure her success by knowing when she was choosing what to eat by what she really wanted, rather than by how many calories she would have to count. It felt achievable to her because she enrolled in a support program so that she didn't have to do it alone. It felt realistic mostly because spending the next 40 years of her life counting calories no longer felt like a realistic option. And because the program offered ongoing support, she didn't feel like the timing was going to be rushed.

But what made this process the S.M.A.R.T.E.S.T. one for Deb? It was special because she was doing something for her brain and body that was coming from love rather than fear. It was motivating because it was the first time in four decades she had considered doing the opposite of what clearly wasn't working. It was aspirational because she hoped to no longer feel imprisoned by every bite, by "good days" and "bad days", and by wondering what in her closet would and wouldn't fit. It was resonant since one of her core values is fun (and thinking about enjoying food surely felt fun!).

It was timely because she was struggling with another cycle of ups and downs, and she didn't want to go through that any longer. It was energizing because she was excited to imagine a short-term and long-term scenario in which food was her friend rather than her foe. She made it simple by not taking on any other personal health goals at the same time—this was the only thing she focused on. And she trusted herself in the process because she knew that she was making the right and healthy choice for herself for right now.

At the time of the writing of this book, it's been two years since Deb took on this goal. Yes, her clothing size is bigger than it was when she was measuring and tracking every bite she ate. Yes, she is sometimes tempted to "try one more time" to shrink herself into old clothing that used to fit. But more importantly, she has yet to give in to that temptation. She has a new closet of clothing in beautiful colors and fabrics that make her feel pretty and (usually) confident. She doesn't calculate what she can have for dinner based on what she ate—or didn't eat—for breakfast and lunch. And she is ready, willing, and able to offer direction and support to anyone else on this journey, or for whatever journey they've chosen for their own mental and physical wellbeing.

HELP STRATEGY 20
ACTION PLANNING

Billie Jean King, the American tennis player who fought for equal prize money for female athletes, once remarked, "Champions keep playing until they get it right."

And part of getting it right—whether it's winning a tennis match or landing a new client—is making a plan. But planning isn't always easy, especially if someone is overwhelmed and keeps thinking to themselves, *What am I supposed to do next?*

As a colleague, parent, or partner, you can play an important role in helping them build a bridge from goal setting to goal attainment. That's where action planning comes in—and we often think we're doing it when we're not.

Does this sound familiar?

Your direct report: "I need to be more consistent at logging my sales calls, so that I have better data for follow-up."

You: "That sounds like a smart idea. Let me know if you need my help."

If so, you may be offering an open-door policy, but you're not actually helping them transform a goal into action.

This is more helpful:

Your direct report: "I need to be more consistent at logging my sales calls, so that I have better data for follow-up."

You: "That sounds like a strategic idea. What's your plan for putting that into action?"

Notice that you don't have to offer *your* action plan to be helpful. You just need to get curious about what *their* action plan is.

When you help someone develop their own action plan, they're much more likely to commit to action steps they come up with themselves rather than ones you've suggested. So while you might think of helping them as *you are making* the plan, consider that you might be even more helpful by supporting them as they design their own plan.

When her kids were starting elementary school, Deb would help Jake and Sophie make a plan of getting homework done. She would have them take a snack, grab their books, and get the work done right away so that they could relax. But by the time they were in second grade, Deb just needed to ask, "What's the homework plan?" after school. As much as she had an opinion about what the homework plan *should* be, she had a stronger belief that they needed to develop their own way of getting it done. Or else, she would be in charge of supervising a homework plan for the next decade—a role she definitely didn't want!

This is true at work as well. Michael Bungay Stanier, the author of *The Advice Trap*, *The Coaching Habit*, and *Do More Great Work*, asks managers to reflect on what's more important: "You being right, having the best idea, or giving the person you are leading the opportunity to come up with their own idea, doing their own thinking, and claiming ownership of their own insight?"

If you want your colleagues or kids (or others) to own their actions, they need to come up with those actions themselves—and with your support.

Actions can be both tangible and intangible—and both kinds add value.

Tangible actions can be observed, quantified, and verified. These are visible actions that have a beginning, a middle, and an end.

There are also invisible, intangible actions someone can take which can lead to tremendous growth, learning, and insight. And often, the two are happening concurrently.

TANGIBLE ACTIONS	INTANGIBLE ACTIONS
Calling an expert to ask for help	Being willing to ask for help
Applying for an open position	Getting comfortable with risk taking
Handing in an assignment on time	Noticing a pattern of behavior
Brainstorming 20 new ideas	Being open to new perspectives
Paying a big invoice	Managing money anxiety
Developing evaluation criteria	Withholding immediate judgment

While you might not be able to "see" the person you're helping take intangible actions, you should trust that they can often result in deep, sustainable change that fundamentally shifts their behavior and performance for the better.

Regardless of whether the actions are visible or invisible, here are ten questions to ask others to help them make a plan and take action.

- Get specific: "What are you planning to do next?"
- Get positive: "What's already working for you in this process?"
- Get buy-in: "What's the opportunity here?"
- Get resourceful: "What else do you need to move forward?"
- Get realistic: "What do you need to stop doing to move forward with this?"
- Get collaborative: "Who else do you need to talk with/work with/align with?"
- Get mental: "What's your current mindset?"
- Get tracking: "How will you measure progress?"
- Get prioritizing: "What step, if done first, will make other steps easier?"
- Get on board: "How else can I help?"

These questions may not be quick or easy for your colleague, friend, or family member to answer. It may take them a little time to think through their responses. And, if you get the sense that they need more of a directive approach—especially if certainty is more important right now than commitment or creativity—you can help by answering these questions with them or for them. So, for example, rather than asking someone who is new to a task, "What else do you need to move forward?" (which they probably can't know yet), your helping strategy might be telling them, "Here's what else you'll need to move forward…"

An Irish proverb shares, "You'll never plough a field by turning it over in your mind." By helping others reflect on their action plan, and then plan to take action, they'll have a clearer, more committed path to getting their goals accomplished.

HELP STRATEGY **21**
ANTICIPATING AND OVERCOMING OBSTACLES

Facing obstacles, roadblocks, and hurdles are a given in work and life. Every single one of us has had to face, and overcome, personal and professional challenges that threaten to derail us from our goals.

And while we often struggle with these interferences alone, we also know that having someone in our corner to help us anticipate and navigate these can be life-changing. You can be that person for your colleagues, friends, and family.

It's tempting to get swept up in the momentum of goal setting and action planning, but real roadblocks can derail even the best laid plans. You can be a thought-partner, cheerleader, and advocate for others as they face potential barriers to forward movement.

A simple and effective way to help someone anticipate what might get in their way is to ask them.

Like what? Like this:

Your partner: "I'm constantly playing catch-up at work and at home. Ever since I've been working remotely, I have distractions on both ends. And I don't feel like I'm doing either job—as a parent and as a team member—as well as I used to. It's exhausting."

You: "I see how exhausted you are. You have some commitments here and at work that are competing with each other. What are those competing commitments?"

Your partner: "Being an attentive parent. Being a supportive partner to you. Contributing to my team. Moving the business forward. Supporting my direct reports. Upskilling. And having even a moment for myself."

By offering your partner the space to reflect on and articulate what's really getting in the way, they can also consider a plan to manage it.

Anticipating and overcoming obstacles with your adult daughter may be as simple as asking, "What could get in the way here?" as she navigates a long-distance relationship. Or you might acknowledge known obstacles in your organization, and ask your team member for a plan, like, "We both know that getting approvals usually takes longer than we expect. How might you accommodate that?" Or, you might be most helpful by pointing out obstacles that your friend might miss, such as, "Your ex-wife is often late when she comes to pick up the kids from your house. Let's plan to meet for dinner at 8:30 rather than 8, so you have some wiggle room."

Common roadblocks include time management, overcoming habits and patterns, breaking through self-limiting beliefs, getting others on board, using demotivating language (for themselves or others), cultivating patience, and even physical and mental health problems.

And helping someone see what might get in their way of achieving their goals is a tool for being a good colleague or friend. But how can we help when the person already sees what's in their way, and decides to quit before they even begin?

HELP STRATEGY ❷❷
POINT OUT "SOLUTION AVERSION"

Anticipating and overcoming obstacles might also include helping someone recognize when they may be engaging in "solution aversion"—a cognitive bias that crops up when we have a sense that the solution to getting something handled may be harder, take longer, or be more complicated than we really want to deal with. When that happens, we minimize the impact of the problem so that we don't have to tackle a tough solution—and that's a roadblock to forward movement.

For example, when Deb's friend Ayelet was considering leaving her frustrating, go-nowhere job in public relations to become a Foreign Service Officer, she began researching the process. Once she realized that there were multiple steps to the process, and that it could take longer than a year and a half to complete it (without any guarantee that she would get a desirable post), she started convincing herself that her current job was good enough. "Public relations is a perfectly acceptable career," she told Deb. "Right?"

The issue wasn't whether Ayelet was right or wrong. It was that the magnitude of the solution was so big and would take so long that she decided the problem wasn't really a problem. Even though it was.

So, if you hear your colleague, friend, or family member minimizing the size or scope of a problem, you can help them by asking whether they might be concerned about the size or scope of the solution. And then, remember to empathize (Help Strategy #5) with them rather than say "you're making too big a deal of this", "don't exaggerate" or "you've done harder things than this!" This is a great opportunity to summon their strengths (Help Strategy #8) to remind them who they are when they're at their best.

HELP STRATEGY ㉓
CHALLENGE CATASTROPHIC THINKING

Deb's most frequent roadblock for many years was catastrophic thinking. Catastrophizing is when you overestimate the likelihood of awful events, and/or overestimate the awfulness of events, and/or underestimate your ability to deal with those events should they happen.

It's exhausting to be a catastrophic thinker, and it's also exhausting to live or work with one of them.

Deb knows this dynamic first-hand. When her kids were little, every time she put them on the school bus, she truly believed it was the last time she would ever see them. Every time she called her husband Michael and the call went to voicemail, she assumed he was dead. Whenever a client didn't call her back immediately, she assumed she was about to lose their business. Deb eventually learned that talking about terrible things all the time wasn't good for her marriage, or her other relationships. She also realized that living this way was unsustainable, and sought professional help. Through therapy and medication, Deb is now living successfully managing regular, mundane worries rather than with debilitating fear.

Admittedly, it can be draining to help someone who catastrophizes. It might also be the kind of situation where you recommend someone get professional help. What you shouldn't do is tell someone "Don't worry about it" or "Things always work out for the best" or ask "What are you making such a big deal about?" All of these are minimizing, and none of these are supportive.

Here are some questions you can ask instead:

- What is the catastrophe you're worried about?
- On a scale of 1–100, how awful would it be?
- Has this awful thing happened to you before?
- How likely is it to happen now?
- What would be the worst possible outcome?
- What would be the best possible outcome?
- What would your most helpful friend or family member say to you about your concern?

Take note that you can use these questions with yourself, too!

HELP STRATEGY 24
REFLECT ON BLIND SPOTS

Sometimes, you'll need to hold a mirror up to someone to help them anticipate and plan for how they might get in their *own* way. As Pulitzer Prize-winning author Junot Diaz wrote: "We all have a blind spot and it's shaped exactly like us."

What is a blind spot? It's a lack of awareness or insight about an area of your behavior or personality. Blind spots tend to be persistent rather than fleeting. And, over time, they can limit what you believe, hinder how you think, narrow your range of behaviors, and ultimately reduce your effectiveness.

Here are some questions you can ask to bring insight to your friend, family member, or colleague's potential blind spots:

- What's your biggest concern?
- What are you hoping **won't** change?
- How much of your time will this take?
- What will you have to postpone to take this on?
- What will you have to say no to?
- Who else do you need to get on board?
- What resources might be hard to get?
- I heard you say you were tired/frustrated/confused a few minutes ago. How will that impact these plans?

And, if you have a close personal or professional relationship with the other person, you might ask for permission to point out a blind spot you've noticed that could impede their success.

When Deb's husband Michael pointed out a blind spot of hers—that every summer she would announce that she would be working a reduced schedule, but then say yes to as many work engagements as any other time of the year—the feedback was both painful and helpful. Not only didn't she see this pattern of behavior, she also didn't see the impact it had on Michael, who was looking forward to spending extra time together. It undermined her credibility, and made her seem unreliable when it came to planning.

Once Michael pointed this out to Deb, she began to anticipate the obstacles that would get in her way to honoring this commitment, such as wanting to please her clients. And most importantly, by planning for them, she could start to create strategies to handle them.

HELP STRATEGY ㉕
ENCOURAGE COMMITMENT AND ACCOUNTABILITY

We all know Nike's famous motto, "Just Do It." It's short, to the point, and a clear call to take initiative. In three brief words, it also implies an understanding of human nature—that we're all likely to come up with reasons and justifications for why we can't or won't or don't "just do it." And, in those same three brief words, it's reminding us to make a commitment to ourselves, and to honor that commitment.

As a colleague, parent, partner, or friend, you—like Nike—have an opportunity to help people in dialing down the excuses and dialing up their commitment and accountability to their actions. Without this kind of help, your coworker may say she's ready to have a critical "managing up" conversation with your boss, but never quite get to it. Your adult child may keep searching for the ideal job, rather than one that will be good enough for right now (so that he can be financially independent). Your partner may claim they'll put away their cell phone at dinner, and yet, always find some excuse to have it on them.

But unfortunately, telling your coworker, child, or partner to "just do it" doesn't usually count as helping!

So, what does?

Asking them to clarify their level of commitment, articulate what they are accountable for and by when, reinforce the why, give and get feedback, and if needed, course correct.

Before they wrote either of their coauthored books (of which this is one), Deb and Sophie needed to check in with each other to make sure they were both committed to the process. They also needed to know how to help each other honor their commitments to the writing project and to each other. Without this step, the roadblocks of writing (tedium, time, self-confidence, hard work, etc.) could easily have overtaken them—and you wouldn't be reading this book!

> Here are some questions you can ask to help your colleague, friend, or family member clarify their level of commitment:
>
> On a scale of 1 to 10 how committed are you?
>
> - (If it's not above 8) What would make this a 9 or a 10?
> - What other commitments do you have that might get in the way?
> - How will you stay committed to this when challenges arise?
> - What can I do to help you stay committed? (Remember to only offer the kind of help you're willing and able to commit to.)

And every week, Deb and Sophie clarified what parts of the writing project they were accountable for and by when. Their Monday morning conversations sounded like this:

- What are you going to do next?
- When will it be done?
- What's the best way for me/someone to help you hold yourself accountable?
- What shouldn't I do? ("Don't remind me of the timeline" and "Don't tell me you're worried about my progress" were two recurring themes.)

Despite the fact that Deb and Sophie were both committed and accountable, when they felt uninspired or exhausted (or both), each of them took a few minutes to remember and reinforce the why:

- What about this feels so important?
- How does this tie into your short- and long-term goals?
- What do you think others will benefit from this?
- By doing, what else becomes possible down the road? (Deb and Sophie are looking at you, *The Today Show!*)

It was also helpful for them to plan for feedback along the way. Deb and Sophie felt quite comfortable giving themselves feedback, ranging from, "Mom, you're going to love what I wrote!" to "Soph, I think I need to scrap this whole section and start over." But they also wanted to help each other with direct, honest, and timely feedback:

- What specifically would you like feedback on?
- What should I say if I'm concerned about something?
- What do you hope we'll be celebrating when this is done?

Of course, even with a great partnership, some people might miss a milestone, a deadline, a success metric, or other elements of the plan. (No details will be shared here, but Deb and/or Sophie know who they are.) And when that happens, you can help by noticing and naming what's happening so you can course correct sooner rather than later.

A gentle helping approach might sound like:

- You've missed some deadlines. What's going on?

- It seems like other priorities have become more pressing, and this project has taken a back seat. What's behind that decision?

- From my perspective, the quality isn't what we'd agreed on. How do you see it?

And a more direct helping approach could be:

- This isn't progressing as I'd hoped. Let's stop and regroup.

- You're behind schedule, and it's impacting other people. I need you to share how you'll get back on track by tomorrow.

- When I ask you what's getting in the way, you mention other people as the problem. I'd like to hear how you see your contribution to this.

You might notice that none of these ways of helping include you telling them why you think their commitment is so important (they already know), or you reminding them about times they fell short of their commitment in their past (they also already know this). The goal of this help is to be supportive and let them take the lead. And, if it's the kind of situation where you can't or shouldn't let them take the lead—because they don't have the skill or will, or because the stakes are too high—then don't ask for their commitment; what you're really seeking is compliance.

Deb experienced this firsthand. When her college friend Phil sent her a text around 11:00 pm on a weeknight to ask if she could talk, Deb said yes. Within the first minute of conversation, Deb could hear that her friend was contemplating suicide. Having been educated as a social worker in graduate school and trained in Mental Health First Aid, Deb knew to ask directly if Phil was considering suicide (the answer was yes), and if he had a plan (the answer was no). Deb asked Phil, "Would you please promise me that you will call your psychologist right now, and leave a message—and then call me right back?" Deb was asking for compliance in this scenario, and it felt like the right thing to ask for at the moment.

Phil complied, left that message with his doctor, and called Deb back. They stayed on the phone for the next hour until Phil felt certain that he was no longer considering harming himself. The next morning, Phil texted Deb to share that he had an appointment later that day. And that text came out of his commitment to Deb—not out of compliance.

Helping our friends, family, and colleagues take initiative, make commitments and stay accountable can feel challenging, especially if we see ourselves as nice, want to be liked, and also want to be encouraging. Nevertheless, supporting others to become more self-directed and self-motivated is exactly what helpers do—even when it's uncomfortable.

As TV screenwriter and producer Shonda Rhimes explained, "It's hard work that makes things happen. It's hard work that creates change."

And helping people change for the better is one of the best ways you can show up for someone.

CHAPTER 10: REVIEW AND REFLECT

REVIEW:

- When helping someone set a goal, think S.M.A.R.T. and S.M.A.R.T.E.S.T. to encourage alignment, engagement, and commitment.

- A vital part of planning and executing is helping someone anticipate roadblocks that could hinder their progress. These roadblocks can be internal or external.

- To help someone stay committed and accountable, reinforce their why.

REFLECT:

- Who do you know who has a goal, but isn't making progress? How could you help them redesign the goal, name the roadblocks, or increase their commitment and accountability?

- What is a goal you have that isn't working for you? What kind of help do you need to recalibrate and move forward? Who will you ask to support you?

CHAPTER 11:

EVALUATE AND CELEBRATE

One of the best ways we can help our colleagues, friends, and family members get better at anything that's important to them is to give them feedback, or to help them evaluate themselves.

And then, we can compound our helpful approach by celebrating their wins with them.

As Daniel Pink, author of *Drive: The Surprising Truth about What Motivates Us*, remarked: "When we make progress and get better at something, it is inherently motivating. In order for people to make progress, they have to get feedback and information on how they're doing."

Feedback can reveal everything from small yet significant wins to big blind spots, and much in between. Without evaluation, you can't calibrate your efforts, check your progress, course correct, or even celebrate what you've accomplished.

And yet, as anyone who has ever heard a sentence that started with "May I give you some feedback?" knows, being evaluated doesn't always feel helpful.

If you've ever received feedback that hurt, you're not imagining it. When we feel like we are being attacked, we really *do* experience pain. It's a form of social rejection, and social rejection can sting—a lot.

So, one way we can help is by giving feedback to others skillfully. Another way of helping is by evaluating both the process and the performance. We can also support others in their own self-evaluation processes. And it should go without saying (but rarely does), that you can be especially helpful by creating the space for your friends and colleagues to celebrate at the finish line—and at milestones along the way.

One important helping tip: Ask "May I offer you some feedback on [insert topic here]?" before offering feedback. Catching someone by surprise or having them worry about what the feedback is about doesn't set either of you up for a productive conversation.

HELP STRATEGY 26
OFFER HELPFUL FEEDBACK

Helpful feedback follows 5 C's: *Contextual, Conversational, Clear, Caring, and Culturally Aware.*

To give feedback that is *contextual*, be clear about why you are giving them the feedback and why you are giving it *now*. If it's anything other than to help them change something that isn't working, or do more of what is working, then you're probably not really helping.

Feedback should also be *conversational*—make it a dialogue, not a monologue. Tell the other person that you see this as a conversation, and that you're open to their perspective, point of view, and position. And then remember to stop talking, and ask them to contribute their ideas.

To be *clear* in giving feedback, be specific about what behavior you're observing, and make sure that you don't confuse a behavior with an *interpretation* of that behavior. For example, "thoughtless" is an interpretation. It could mean just about anything. Compare that with "You don't respond to my emails within the week" or "You interrupt me when we have friends over for dinner," which are behaviors.

Demonstrating *caring* is additionally important. Check in during the conversation to see whether your message is coming across the way you intend. And if not, stop talking and address the gap before you continue giving feedback. "I'm hoping you hear this as helpful and supportive," you might say, "but let me stop for a moment and check in with you about how this is landing. How are you feeling about this feedback?" This shows that you care about the whole person.

Finally, bring *cultural awareness* to your conversation. Communication styles differ across cultures, and you may want to consider how to adapt your approach—especially within a global company. For example, as a native New Yorker, Deb can be very direct in giving feedback, but when she taught Executive Communications in Beijing, she discovered that many of her MBA students came from a culture that prefers a less direct, and much softer approach. While you don't have to change who you are, even small shifts can make a big difference.

By putting the feedback into context, making it conversational, being clear and caring, and showing cultural awareness, you have a significant role in making feedback have a positive impact for your colleagues, friends, and family.

HELP STRATEGY 27
EVALUATE BOTH PROCESS AND PERFORMANCE

Deb comes from a long line of impressive musicians. Her great-uncle Dave, a violist, was at one time the longest playing musician in the history of the New York Metropolitan Opera. His younger brother, Sol, was a prolific musical composer. Deb's grandmother was a pianist (as well as a nurse), and her father plays most string instruments, from autoharp and banjo to guitar and piano.

With this impressive bloodline, Deb was four years old when she began taking piano lessons—and quickly showed her prowess. She began transposing songs from major to minor keys by the age of five, composed a range of original melodies shortly after, and taught herself to play her favorite 80's pop songs by the age of 11.

When she was 12, Deb's dad put a piece of sheet music in front of her that he wanted them to duet together—a four-hand Mozart sonata. "Will you play it for me first?" Deb asked. "No, let's learn it together," he replied.

And that's when Deb's eight-year-long secret was revealed: she had never learned to read music. She could only play by ear. As a result, her ability to learn new, more complex musical compositions stalled—and then she quit playing altogether.

Had Deb's piano teacher helped evaluate her *process* of learning to play piano, and not just her *performance*, Deb would likely have learned to read music. But, because Deb was able to coast on her ear for music, and nobody noticed, she can now only play what she remembers from age 12. (But if you love Cindy Lauper, Culture Club, and Wham!, then you're in luck.)

Whether you're offering feedback or supporting something through the process of self-evaluation, it helps to distinguish the *what* from the *how*. It gives the person you're helping additional opportunities to evaluate, recalibrate, and celebrate.

Imagine that you and your team member worked hard on a client pitch, but the client chose a different agency. You might say:

"I know you're disappointed that we didn't land this client. I also want to acknowledge how thoughtful and creative your approach was in planning this pitch. You really thought outside the box!"

In this case, you might not be able to celebrate the what (landing the client), but you can positively acknowledge the how (how creative the pitch was). This will help encourage your coworker to apply that innovative thinking again.

Or imagine that your son makes you and your partner dinner for your anniversary, and leaves the kitchen a disaster. You might say:

"The chicken picatta was exactly the way I like it—very lemony. However, the fact that you left all the dishes, pots, and pans dirty made it hard for me to relax and enjoy this meal."

So high marks for the what (chicken), and low marks for the how (clean-up). This will help remind your son to think about what also matters to you, like cleanliness, and not having extra work to do (and yes, you may have to remind him more than once!).

HELP STRATEGY 28
HELP THEM SEE THEIR PROGRESS

If you are like most people, you may find it difficult to complete a task or reach a goal if you can't see the progress you are making along the way. It can be agonizing to have to guess how far you've come, how well you're doing, or what you have left to do to reach your goal.

Imagine your computer is restarting.

Picture that little green bar that tells you how much longer your computer will take to boot up. It moves slowly, but as long as you see progress, you can relax a bit. Now imagine your computer is restarting but it doesn't give you any indication of how much longer it will take or what percent complete it is. That would be miserable!

All of us need checkpoints to tell us how we are doing. Without indication of progress, it can be difficult to stay motivated.

When Sophie started college, she noticed that, in many of her courses, she didn't know what her grades looked like because there was no progress update from her professors. In high school, she always knew where she stood. Each test and paper grade was put online so she could figure out what her final grade might look like. Sophie found it challenging in college to stay motivated to work through the end of the semester because there were very few checkpoints for her where she could see her progress. Did she have an A? Did she have a C? Was she studying the right way for tests? Were her papers written the way her professor wanted them? She really didn't know.

This is not an issue that Sophie faces alone. Maybe your boss doesn't give you consistent feedback on your progress, so you don't ever really know how close you are to meeting expectations. (Or maybe you are that boss, and your direct reports are waiting to hear from you how they're progressing.)

Shirley Chisholm, the first black woman elected to the United States Congress, commented: "You don't make progress by standing on the sidelines, whimpering and complaining. You make progress by implementing ideas." And you don't help someone by ignoring their progress while you wait for completion; you help them by acknowledging what they've implemented along the way.

Some forms of progress are more visible than others, but that doesn't mean you should only address what you can see. You might be able to see that your friend has gained muscle tone in her upper arms, but you might not notice that her blood pressure is now in a healthy range. You might be able to see that your colleague is halfway done implementing new customer relationship management software, but you might not notice that he is conquering his fear of technology head-on.

So one helpful approach is to name the progress that you can clearly see. "I notice that you've been waking up early most mornings to exercise before work. I'm impressed with your commitment!"

Another strategy is to ask them what you don't see, but they do: "Where else are you progressing that I might not see?"

You can also point them in the direction of acknowledging small changes they've made along the way. "What have you stopped doing that's been helpful?" "What have you started doing?" "What have you kept doing because it's been working?"

When it comes to helping others see their progress, stop staring at the finish line, and start cheering from the sidelines.

HELP STRATEGY 29
INVITE SELF-EVALUATION

South African poet, philosopher, songwriter, and philanthropist Gift Gugu Mona remarked, "Your mind is like a gold mine; if you dig deep, you will find something golden."

One of the best ways we can help others is by encouraging them to dig deep themselves. By prompting them to reflect on their own process, progress, and performance, we can help them discover some "golden nuggets" that they can use to move forward.

Yes, you could tell your daughter that you think she could have handled the tough conversation with her soccer coach a bit better. And, you could ask her: "What do you think you did well in your conversation with your coach?" and "What would you have done differently?"

This way, she owns her choices, and the impacts of those choices.

Yes, you could tell your direct report that you think his delegation (or lack thereof) is a problem. And you can also ask: "What do you think is hindering you in getting things done on time?" or even, "What's hardest for you about delegating?"

This way, he can reflect on his own skill sets, and be an active participant in improving. Or, if you notice that his delegation self-evaluation is dramatically different from how you see his skills, you can decide to address that, too.

You can invite someone to evaluate themselves before tackling a tough project, during a personal change, or after a hard conversation. And, it can be especially helpful to encourage self-awareness after what author Tasha Eurich calls "alarm clock events." In her book *Insight: The Surprising Truth about How Others See Us, How We See Ourselves, and Why the Answers Matter More than You Think*, Eurich contends that we can increase our internal self-awareness (how we see ourselves) and external self-awareness (how others see us) in these three situations that open our eyes to important truths about ourselves.

1. New rules or roles: By stretching our comfort zones and increasing the demands placed on us, we can "super-charge our self-knowledge."

2. Earthquake: When we experience a significant or severe event, we can learn much about ourselves by how we react and respond.

3. Everyday insight: It doesn't have to take a massive change for us to learn about ourselves. We might overhear an offhand

comment or get a piece of praise that alerts us to how we're doing.

Self-evaluation is invaluable. It taps into your colleague's, friend's, or family member's own familiarity with their work, situation, relationships, and environment, since they're the ones really involved in the day to day. It gives people the opportunity to examine the gaps between what they're trying to do, and how it's actually going—and celebrate when it's going exactly the way they'd hoped. It can make it easier for people to own their setbacks and tricky experiences (since they aren't defending themselves against someone else's evaluation), and learn from them. Self-evaluation gives people the space to reflect on how they're feeling, not just what they're doing. It can lead to more committed changes, rather than just compliant ones.

And self-evaluation gives *you* the opportunity to see how self-aware they are of the impact they're having on themselves, and others.

Here are some questions you can ask to encourage self-evaluation:

- What are you doing well?
- What are you most proud of?
- What could you do better?
- What would you do differently next time?
- What do you want or need to learn?
- What are you learning about yourself?
- What are you learning that you'll apply down the road?
- What changes are you prepared to make?
- What are you celebrating?

By encouraging self-evaluation, you can help people become lifelong students of themselves. As Louisa May Alcott wrote in *Little Women:* "I am not afraid of storms, for I am learning how to sail my ship."

HELP STRATEGY ❸⓪
PROMOTE THE PAUSE

Activist and artist Brandon Kyle Goodman shared on Twitter: "I told my friend that I'm emotionally 'hitting a wall' and she said 'Sometimes walls are there so we can lean on them and rest.' I can't even begin to express how much I needed to hear this."

So much of how you help others is offering them support and direction to keep going.

And yet, sometimes the best thing you can do is give them the space to stop. Stop trying to control something they can't control. Stop trying to change something that isn't changing. Stop trying to help someone who doesn't want their help. Stop doing something that isn't working. Stop doing something even though they've always done it that way. Stop moving forward without asking "what do I want?", "where am I trying to go?", "is this working?", and "what is this costing me?"

Offering someone a pause is an opportunity for them to reflect and recalibrate rather than pursue a course of action that may not be going in the right direction. Deb paused when her lifelong yo-yo dieting wasn't achieving what she wanted. Sophie paused her pursuit of a basketball career when her doctor told her she wouldn't be taller than five feet. After that, Sophie started racewalking, and after three years of training for national competitions, she paused so that she could write her book and focus on her college education. And, in the 2020/2021 Tokyo Olympics, the world's most decorated gymnast Simone Biles stepped out of competition when she knew that her mental health might jeopardize her physical safety.

Here are some examples that might sound familiar:

- Your friend might need to pause to recalibrate her expectations for becoming an empty-nester when she realized that it was harder than she'd expected.

- Your boss might need to pause to reconsider whether she should keep saying yes to a seemingly unsatisfiable client.

- You may need to pause to reflect on whether helping your elderly mom stay at home rather than enter a care facility is really helping.

When you notice someone hitting a wall, you might encourage them to figure out a way over it, around it, under it, or through it.

Or you can promote the idea of taking a pause to reconsider and make a new plan.

HELP STRATEGY 31
CELEBRATE

Let's play a round of Jeopardy. The answer is "ice cream." What's the question?

"What is Deb and Sophie's favorite way to celebrate?"

Let's play a second round. The answer is "a party." What's the question?

"What is Deb and Sophie's least favorite way to celebrate?"

(Unless it's an ice cream party—and then they'll figure it out.)

Celebrating successes is important—and often overlooked. Why isn't celebration a regular part of our professional and personal plans?

Many of us skip celebrating and move on to the next item on our agenda to get done. Who has time to run a victory lap when there are still budgets to balance, clients to please, and dinners to get on the table?

As Sloane Crosley writes in *I Was Told There'd Be Cake:* "People are less quick to applaud you as you grow older. Life starts out with everyone clapping when you take a poo and goes downhill from there."

We often feel like celebration should be "saved" for the big wins: a graduation from college, landing a new multimillion dollar customer, a significant promotion. And, since these are often few and far between, we don't acknowledge the smaller victories, like getting your boss to approve your flexible work schedule, or your baby sleeping more than four hours at a stretch, or realizing that you didn't yell when your daughter missed curfew... again.

One concern that Deb has heard from a number of the leaders she works with is: "If I celebrate every win, I'm worried that my team members will become dependent on recognition."

What managers *should* be worried about is losing people due to lack of celebration than retaining people who really, truly crave it. Almost 80% of US employees who leave their job cite feeling under-appreciated as the reason; 65% of employees claim they've received no recognition within the last year; and 35% explicitly note that this under-appreciation negatively impacts their productivity. And 78% say they would work harder if they were given more recognition.

Why is this so important?

According to Judith Glaser, author of *Conversational Intelligence: How Great Leaders Build Trust and Get Extraordinary Results*, celebrating success helps us feel included, bonded, and appreciated. Celebration drives belonging and collaboration, and lays the foundation for creativity, calm, increased focus and resilience to stress—even during periods of high pressure.

Celebration is motivating, inspiring, and educational. It reminds us that we're worthy of positive time, energy, and attention. It helps us get on track to face hard things, and stay on track when things get even harder.

Those all sound like things to celebrate!

You can help the people you work with and live with leverage those benefits by reminding them to celebrate, and helping them to do so—whether the victory is big or small, and whether or not there's still work to be done.

Here are a few ideas of what to help your friends, family, and colleagues celebrate:

- Achieving a personal or professional milestone
- Deciding to take a much-needed pause on the path to a personal or professional milestone
- Starting a new project or challenge
- Navigating a tricky interpersonal relationship artfully
- Ending a toxic relationship
- Achieving a first or another win
- Honoring their own boundaries
- Saying no

- Taking something off their plate
- Attempting something scary
- Learning from a setback or mistake
- Embodying their company's, family's, or own core values
- Getting to the halfway mark
- Changing an embedded habit or behavior
- Positively impacting someone else.

And how, exactly, should you celebrate someone—or help them to celebrate themselves?

The way *they* would want to be celebrated.

You can certainly ask them, "How would you like to celebrate?" And you can also think about where they fall on these continua, based on your prior experience with them:

Big deal (like a vacation) ⟷ Small deal (like a nice dinner out)

Public acknowledgement (like an announcement in the company newsletter) ⟷ Private acknowledgement (like a handwritten note)

For them alone (like a massage gift certificate) ⟷ With others (like a bagel brunch with the team)

Fun (like an ice cream party) ⟷ Serious (like a donation made in their name)

Tangible perk/treat (like flowers) ⟷ Intangible rewards (like your gratitude)

(In case you'd like to celebrate Deb and Sophie for writing this book, Deb would like fresh flowers, coffee chip ice cream, a gift card for a massage, or a donation made in her name to an organization that supports LGBTQIA+ causes. Sophie would prefer a fully-funded trip to the thrift store, pizza, or a donation to a local animal shelter.)

When you help someone celebrate—whether it's a reminder to celebrate themselves, or you celebrate with and for them—you are supporting them in acknowledging their progress. You are giving them the opportunity to stop and take stock of where they've been and where they are now. And you are helping them to see that they really, truly matter.

CHAPTER 11: REVIEW AND REFLECT

 REVIEW:

- You can help someone assess their progress by offering them helpful feedback, as well as by giving them the opportunity to self-evaluate.

- Taking a break should be viewed as a healthy and necessary way to check in with yourself, assess your mindsets and behaviors, and decide what to do next. Invite the people you're helping to pause every now and then.

- Celebrating is an important part of acknowledging progress and achievement. Make sure that you celebrate someone the way *they* want to be recognized, not the way you do.

 REFLECT:

- Who could use some celebrating right now? What will you do to make that happen?

- What do you want to celebrate for yourself? How would you like to celebrate? And who would you like to help you do this?

AFTERWORD

Getting better at helping others—and yourself—can make work and life easier and more fulfilling. It can improve our relationships up, down, and across our organizations. It can make caring for and being cared for by our family members less frustrating and more equitable. And it can make being there for one another with friends feel like a boost rather than a burden.

Offering, asking for, and accepting help is exactly what we need in order to keep up with our ever-changing world. And since things are becoming more complex, here's this whole book simplified to three core questions:

Offering help: "What kind of help would be most helpful to you?"

Asking for help: "Are you willing and able to help me?"

Accepting help: "Am I willing to accept the help being offered to me?"

Please know that our offer to help you doesn't end with this book. Please feel free to reach out to us at Authors@GoToHelpBook. com. The answer is YES (even if that means we connect you to a resource that isn't one of us).

Thank you for reading, and for helping us all get better at helping each other.

Deborah Grayson Riegel and Sophie Riegel

ABOUT THE AUTHORS

Deborah Grayson Riegel is an executive coach, keynote speaker and consultant. She has taught leadership communication for Wharton Business School, Columbia Business School, and Duke Corporate Education. She is a regular contributor for *Harvard Business Review, Inc., Psychology Today, Forbes,* and *Fast Company.* The author of *Overcoming Overthinking: 36 Ways to Tame Anxiety for Work, School, and Life,* she consults and speaks for clients including Amazon, BlackRock, Bloomberg, Johnson & Johnson, PepsiCo, and The United States Army. Her work has been featured in worldwide media, including *The Wall Street Journal, Bloomberg Businessweek, The New York Times* and *Oprah Magazine.*

Sophie Riegel is an undergraduate student at Duke University. She is the author of *Don't Tell Me To Relax!: One Teen's Journey to Survive Anxiety (And How You Can Too)*, and *Overcoming Overthinking: 36 Ways to Tame Anxiety for Work, School, and Life*. She is a mental health advocate who speaks across the globe about her experiences, and has been featured on the Tamron Hall Show, Thrive Global, the Times of Israel, PsychCentral, and more. She recorded a TED Talk in 2020 about how to reduce the stigma of mental illness, and looks forward to continuing to encourage conversations about mental health.

Made in the USA
Monee, IL
26 January 2022